T0328663

Cambridge Elements ≡

Elements in Psycholinguistics
edited by
Paul Warren
Victoria University of Wellington

GRAMMATICAL ENCODING FOR SPEECH PRODUCTION

Linda Ruth Wheeldon
University of Agder

Agnieszka Konopka
University of Aberdeen

CAMBRIDGE
UNIVERSITY PRESS

CAMBRIDGE
UNIVERSITY PRESS

Shaftesbury Road, Cambridge CB2 8EA, United Kingdom

One Liberty Plaza, 20th Floor, New York, NY 10006, USA

477 Williamstown Road, Port Melbourne, VIC 3207, Australia

314–321, 3rd Floor, Plot 3, Splendor Forum, Jasola District Centre, New Delhi – 110025, India

103 Penang Road, #05–06/07, Visioncrest Commercial, Singapore 238467

Cambridge University Press is part of Cambridge University Press & Assessment, a department of the University of Cambridge.

We share the University's mission to contribute to society through the pursuit of education, learning and research at the highest international levels of excellence.

www.cambridge.org
Information on this title: www.cambridge.org/9781009264556

DOI: 10.1017/9781009264518

First published 2023

A catalogue record for this publication is available from the British Library.

ISBN 978-1-009-26455-6 Paperback
ISSN 2753-9768 (online)
ISSN 2753-975X (print)

Grammatical Encoding for Speech Production

Elements in Psycholinguistics

DOI: 10.1017/9781009264518
First published online: March 2023

Linda Ruth Wheeldon
University of Agder

Agnieszka Konopka
University of Aberdeen

Author for correspondence: Linda Ruth Wheeldon, linda.r.wheeldon@uia.no

Abstract: During the production of spoken sentences, the linearisation of a 'thought' is accomplished via the process of grammatical encoding, that is, the building of a hierarchical syntactic frame that fixes the linear order of lexical concepts. While much research has demonstrated the independence of lexical and syntactic representations, exactly what is represented remains a matter of dispute. Moreover, theories differ in terms of whether words or syntax drive grammatical encoding. This debate is also central to theories of the time-course of grammatical encoding. Speaking is usually a rapid process in which articulation begins before an utterance has been entirely planned. Current theories of grammatical encoding make different claims about the scope of grammatical encoding prior to utterance onset, and the degree to which planning scope is determined by linguistic structure or by cognitive factors. The authors review current theories of grammatical encoding and evaluate them in light of relevant empirical evidence. This title is also available as Open Access on Cambridge Core.

Keywords: speaking, language production, grammatical encoding, structural priming, planning scope

ISBNs: 9781009264556 (PB), 9781009264518 (OC)
ISSNs: 2753-9768 (online), 2753-975X (print)

Contents

1 Introduction

Psycholinguistic and linguistic theory agree that sentence production is a generative process involving a separate lexicon and grammar (e.g., Chomsky, 1965; Levelt, 1989). Speakers of a language can retrieve words from their mental lexicon and order them in accordance with their grammar to generate a theoretically infinite number of sentences. This potential for unbounded creativity is at variance with the evidence, to be reviewed in what follows, that spoken language tends toward repetition. Nevertheless, some degree of separation between lexical and syntactic representations and processes is a cornerstone of all current models of grammatical encoding (e.g., Chang, Dell & Bock, 2006; Dell, Oppenheim & Kittredge, 2008; Levelt, Roelofs & Meyer, 1999). Theoretical approaches to the processes of lexical retrieval and syntactic structure building in fluent sentence production are discussed in Section 1. The theoretical framing will focus on the key dichotomy in the field: whether grammatical encoding is driven by lexical (e.g., Bock & Levelt, 1994) or syntactic representations (e.g., Chang et al., 2006; Dell et al., 2008). We will begin with a theoretical overview, which will incorporate a brief discussion of theories of lexical representation and access (e.g., Wheeldon & Konopka, 2018), before turning to how retrieved lexical items are integrated into the unfolding syntax of an utterance.

We then evaluate the evidence for the independence of syntax from lexical representations and the nature of the structural representations generated during grammatical encoding (Section 2). The critical evidence in this area has been largely derived from studies of structural priming. In the early days of this research, the presence of lexically unsupported syntactic priming was taken as evidence of abstract structural processing in sentence production (e.g., Bock, 1986). Further research demonstrated limited involvement of the lexicon in the generation of syntactic structures. Existing rich evidence from within-language and between-language comparisons largely supports the view of the independence of syntax and the lexicon in adult speakers (Branigan & Pickering, 2017; Chang et al., 2006; Mahowald, James, Futrell & Gibson, 2016; Pickering & Ferreira, 2008), but with outstanding questions remaining in developmental psycholinguistics (e.g., Messenger, Branigan & McLean, 2011; Rowland, Chang, Ambridge, Pine & Lieven, 2012). Priming research has also helped to delimit the nature of the syntactic representations generated during sentence production (e.g., Bernolet, Hartsuiker & Pickering, 2007; Branigan, Pickering, McLean & Stewart, 2006; Ferreira, 2003; Fox Tree & Meijer, 1999; Hardy, Wheeldon & Segaert, 2020; Ziegler, Snedeker & Wittenburg, 2017).

In the next section we switch focus to the time-course of grammatical encoding (Section 3). Here, the theoretical debate turns on whether online sentence planning occurs in a lexically incremental fashion (Bock & Levelt, 1994; Griffin, 2001; Meyer, Sleiderink & Levelt, 1998; also see Meyer, Wheeldon, Van der Meulen & Konopka, 2012) or in a structurally driven, hierarchical fashion (Konopka & Meyer, 2014; Lee, Brown-Schmidt & Watson, 2013; Martin, Miller & Vu, 2004; Momma, 2021; Smith & Wheeldon, 1999; Wheeldon, 2013; Wheeldon, Smith & Apperly 2011). The critical evidence for this debate comes from studies of planning scope in picture description paradigms to determine the degree of planning occurring in advance of articulation onset. These paradigms frequently make use of eye tracking, allowing the time-course of planning from the initial uptake of visual information to the onset of speech to be determined (e.g., Konopka, 2019). More recently, cross-linguistic studies have investigated the role of language-specific grammatical constraints on planning (Allum & Wheeldon, 2007, 2009; Hwang & Kaiser, 2014a; Momma, Slevc & Phillips, 2016; Norcliffe, Konopka, Brown & Levinson, 2015; Sauppe, Norcliffe, Konopka, van Valin & Levinson, 2013).

The Element will also include relevant data from studies of bilingual sentence planning (e.g., Konopka, Meyer & Forest, 2018). This research speaks both to the representation of syntactic structure and to the issue of the effects of cognitive load on planning scope. We will review evidence that grammatical planning scope can be modulated by non-linguistic factors and cognitive limitations, including speed requirements (e.g., Ferreira & Swets, 2002), working memory (e.g., Swets, Jacovina & Gerrig, 2014), and attention (e.g., Jongman, Meyer & Roelofs, 2015; Jongman, Roelofs & Meyer, 2015).

In the final section of the Element (Section 4), we will provide an evaluation of the strengths and weaknesses of the methodological approaches that have been used to date in the field. Finally, we will reassess the theoretical landscape, highlighting gaps and defining the resulting avenues for future research.

1.1 Grammatical Encoding in Speech Production

1.1.1 The Component Processes for Speaking

In this section, we review theories of grammatical encoding for speech production, focusing on the proposed relationship between words and syntax. We begin, however, with setting the process of grammatical encoding in context. All cognitive models of speech production are heavily influenced by Levelt's classic blueprint for the speaker (Levelt, 1989), which in turn built on the seminal work of Garrett (1975). The proposal is that utterances are produced in a number of more-or-less successive processes, and there is also agreement on the broad structure of the processes involved (see Figure 1). The starting

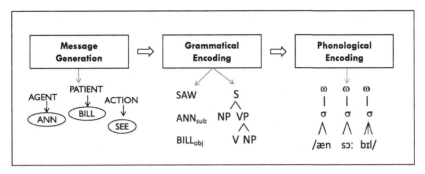

Figure 1 A representation of the key processing stages of spoken sentence production.

point is message generation, which involves the construction of a conceptual representation that details the information that the speaker wants to convey. This representation is usually known as the *message* (Levelt, 1989). The current view is that messages are non-linear and must at least contain conceptual category information. Messages can be very short (e.g., mapping onto utterances like 'Hi' or 'Look there!') or much longer, including a thematic structure which assigns concepts to thematic roles such as agent or patient (e.g., mapping onto utterances like 'The politician was amazed by the volume of fan mail'; see Konopka & Brown-Schmidt, 2014, for a review). In addition, messages should contain information that is required to generate a grammatical sentence including time, mood and focus, as well as any language-specific information required by a language for obligatory syntactic or morphological markers (see Levelt, 1989, chapter 3, for a detailed discussion).

The message triggers grammatical encoding processes, which include selecting the appropriate lexical items, assigning grammatical roles and generating a syntactic structure to fix their linear order. The phonological structure of the utterance is constructed in the subsequent phase, where an abstract prosodic representation is generated which forms the input to phonetic and articulatory processes. Grammatical encoding processes therefore form the link between the conceptual structure to be conveyed and the sound structure of the utterance that will convey it. The component processes are *lexical retrieval* and *syntactic structure building*.

1.1.2 Lexical Retrieval Processes

Lexical retrieval refers to the activation and retrieval of words from the mental lexicon. During production, activation at the conceptual level triggers a lexical search. Psycholinguistic models largely agree that lexical representations exist independently of semantics, at the *lemma* and *lexeme* levels (Kempen & Huijbers, 1983). *Lemmas* are abstract, modality-general and language-specific lexical entries that are activated by information at the conceptual level. In turn, lemma selection activates *lexemes*, that is, representations that include word-form information (see Caramazza & Miozzo, 1997, vs. Roelofs, Meyer & Levelt, 1998), and then phonological encoding processes. For example, a speaker wishing to convey information about one person (a woman) transferring something (a book) to another person (a man) will generate a message-level representation consisting of conceptual nodes that correspond to the nominal concepts *woman, man* and *book*, as well as the action of transferring X to Y, and this information may activate the *lemma* nodes for the nouns 'woman', 'man', 'book' and the verbs 'give' and 'donate'. Lemmas include item-specific syntactic information, such as grammatical gender for nouns and restrictions on syntactic alternations for verbs (e.g., the verb 'give' can be used with both prepositional-object [PO] and double-object [DO] syntax, while the verb 'donate' can only be used with PO syntax).

The majority of models describing lexical access focus on retrieval of individual words – most often nouns (e.g., 'woman', 'man', 'book') – or production of short sequences of words in simple or complex noun phrases (NPs) (e.g., 'the woman', 'the woman and the man'). The likelihood of selecting a lemma and the speed of selecting one noun lemma over another vary as a function of (a) word-specific variables (e.g., lexical frequency, age of acquisition, name agreement), (b) properties of the words' lexical neighbours (e.g., neighbourhood density, recent activation of neighbouring lexical nodes, the degree to which relationships between words are taxonomic or thematic), and (c) the proposed architecture of the production system (e.g., the direction of information flow between the conceptual, lexical and phonological levels). Two classes of models, Levelt and colleagues' serial model (Levelt et al., 1999; also see Roelofs, 1992) and Dell and colleagues' interactive models of lexical access (Dell, 1986; Dell, Schwartz, Martin, Saffran & Gagnon, 1997), have led the theorising in the field. In both models, the concepts or lexical nodes that are most strongly activated are selected for production, but the models differ in the degree to which they allow activation from lower levels to influence selection: serial models assume a feedforward flow of activation from concepts to lemmas and to phonological encoding, while interactive models allow for feedback from lower levels.

Lexical retrieval models also differ in their assumptions about the selection process at the lemma level, specifically the degree to which lemmas do or do not compete for selection (Levelt et al., 1999 vs. Mahon, Costa, Peterson, Vargas & Caramazza, 2007; see Abdel-Rahman & Melinger, 2009, for a review). The predictions of these models are often tested with the picture–word interference paradigm, where speakers name individual pictured objects while ignoring superimposed printed words. Retrieval times normally increase in the presence of semantic competitors, such as when trying to name the picture of a cat while seeing the printed word 'dog', and decrease in the presence of phonological neighbours, such as when trying to name the picture of a cat while seeing the printed word 'cap'. Debates concerning the size and direction of these effects often hinge on determining the joint effects of multiple individual processes: conceptual priming (semantically related words prime each other), lexical interference (taxonomically related words compete against each other for selection), lexical facilitation (thematically related word prime each other) and phonological facilitation (phonologically related words prime each other). Production of a *sequence* of words, either in phrases (e.g., 'the cat and the dog') or without a phrasal context ('cat dog'), naturally multiplies the number of processes to be completed and adds an additional parameter: retrieval of each word (word n) can be influenced by anticipatory activation of word $n+1$, and likewise, retrieval of word $n+1$ is influenced by production of word n. As in most picture-word interference paradigms, retrieval of word n is slower when word $n+1$ is a semantic competitor, but retrieval of word $n+1$ is also slower when word n is a semantic competitor (an effect known as cumulative semantic interference).

In a recent meta-analysis, Bürki, Elbuy, Madec and Vasishth (2020) concluded that existing research does not adjudicate between models assuming competitive and non-competitive lexical access. Oppenheim and Nozari (2021) also showed that behavioural indexes such as the presence of semantic interference or facilitation cannot be used to conclusively distinguish between competitive and non-competitive lexical access, as competitive and non-competitive selection rules can produce similar behavioural outcomes. A more promising approach is to track context-specific changes in retrieval speed in order to model experience-driven changes in activation levels and connections between the conceptual level and word level (see Dell & Jacobs, 2016; Dell, Nozari & Oppenheim, 2014; Oppenheim, Dell & Schwartz, 2010, and Oppenheim & Nozari, 2021, for more detail with supporting empirical evidence and simulations). For example, the degree to which both taxonomically and thematically related distractors interfere with production of a target word depends on the way these relationships are represented in the model, rather than depending on selection rules.

The models of lexical retrieval reviewed in the preceding text are concerned with the nature of lexical representations for content words (mostly nouns) and thus do not make explicit claims about processes responsible for integrating sequences of lexical items into longer utterances. In the rest of the Element, we focus primarily on a different long-standing debate in psycholinguistics – namely, the contribution of the lexicon to grammatical encoding (see Bock, 1982, 1987, for early reviews). This area of research focuses on production of longer, multi-word utterances with complex syntactic structures and, critically, utterances requiring retrieval of verbs.

1.1.3 The Need for Syntax

Producing grammatically correct multi-word utterances requires that words be produced in a specific order, that is, that they be sequenced according to language-specific word-order rules. This sequencing is referred to as linearisation. Interestingly, while it is clear that linguistic utterances *are* structured, the nature of the structural representations generated to output grammatically correct word sequences is debated. This puzzle concerns the degree to which the lexicon is involved in the generation of sentence structure.

Broadly speaking, the generation of sentence structure has been described, in different accounts, as a by-product of lexical retrieval processes or as the outcome of processes operating outside of the lexicon (e.g., see Bock, 1987, for a review). Lexicalist (or functional) accounts propose that there is no strict separation between the lexicon and grammar: speakers retrieve lexical items as required by the preverbal message they want to communicate, and it is the lexical retrieval process that initiates the building of a syntactic structure. In other words, the building of a linguistic structure is dependent on lexical activation. By implication then, syntax is largely epiphenomenal. However, the linearisation of a longer, complex message that requires activation of multiple content words poses a problem for this account, as lemma activation can be responsible for the activation of 'local' syntactic information but is less likely to be responsible for the building of larger syntactic frames (also see Section 3 for a discussion of planning scope in multi-word utterances). Abstract structural accounts are better able to account for linearisation in longer utterances, as they propose that larger *structures* (or *frames*) are built by abstract syntactic procedures independently of the lexical items that will be slotted into them. These procedures are sensitive to word-specific syntactic requirements, but they are not, crucially, triggered by activation of individual lemmas.

The viability of the lexical account, and thus the origins of the debate between lexical and abstract accounts, has historical roots. Language research has been largely skewed in favour of comprehension rather than production, and comprehension studies show strong reliance on the lexicon during parsing. In comprehension, listeners receive a linguistic signal that comes in word by word over time and they must integrate this information to decode the speaker's message. Naturally, given that listeners process incoming information as soon as it becomes available, the processor may give more weight to new lexical information (which can be quickly integrated with those parts of the utterance that have already been heard) than to structural information (as the structural representation of a spoken utterance is built up or inferred from a *string* of words rather than from individual words). Listeners do generate predictions about upcoming words, but evidence of prediction based on the semantic or lexical content of a sentence (be it coarse-grained, i.e., involving entire words, or finer-grained, i.e., involving sublexical units) is currently more plentiful than evidence of prediction of structure based on grammatical markers or parts of speech (see Huettig, Rommers & Meyer, 2011, for a review). Thus, the demands of comprehension for structural processing may be less stringent than in production and may effectively 'hide' potential effects of abstract structural processes. Levels of engagement during comprehension can also vary, such that 'good enough' processing (i.e., the build-up of underspecified representations) may be sufficient for successful comprehension in many contexts (Karimi & Ferreira, 2016). Indeed, finding evidence of the involvement of abstract structural processes in comprehension requires development of more sensitive measurement tools or ensuring greater engagement on the listener's part (see Tooley & Bock, 2014).

In contrast, the distinction between lexical sources of structure and abstract structural processes is more salient and thus more relevant in production. The processing demands of language production on the speaker are arguably higher than the demands of comprehension on the listener. To produce an utterance, speakers must first decide what they want to say (albeit not necessarily in large, sentence-sized chunks) and must then begin generating the linguistic material they will need to communicate their message from scratch. This involves both structural and lexical processing, so stronger reliance on lexical than structural information may not be as viable in production as it is in comprehension: producing a sequence of words cannot bypass structural processing and rely exclusively on lexically specific syntactic information. An empirical challenge in the field of language production is therefore the need to delineate the boundary between lexically driven and lexically free influences on word order, and to explain when and how these processes interact.

1.1.4 Models of Grammatical Encoding: The Relationship between Words and Syntax

Models of grammatical encoding differ in the relationship they propose between words and structure. There are different claims about which level of representation encodes links between lexical and structural information, with some models encoding explicit links between lexical concepts and thematic roles at the conceptual level (e.g., Chang, 2002; Chang et al., 2006), and others in grammatical representations between lemmas and syntactic information, allowing lexical retrieval and structure building to interact during grammatical encoding (e.g., Bock & Levelt, 1994; Cleland & Pickering, 2003, 2006; Ferreira, 2000; Ferreira, Morgan & Slevc, 2018; Levelt, 1989; Levelt et al., 1999; Momma, 2021; Pickering & Branigan, 1998). Models also diverge in the degree to which lexical or structural information guide grammatical encoding.

The earliest models of grammatical encoding were lexically driven and accorded a central role to lemma representations, which comprised semantic and syntactic-lexical information (e.g., Bock & Levelt, 1994; for reviews, see Bock & Ferreira, 2014; Ferreira & Slevc, 2007; Ferreira et al., 2018). Later versions of this approach limited lemmas to encoding aspects of lexical syntax, including grammatical category (e.g., noun, verb, adjective) as well as syntactic features (e.g., tense, number, grammatical gender; e.g., Levelt et al., 1999, see also Roelofs & Ferreira, 2019). These models also assume a discrete flow of information, with lemma selection occurring during grammatical encoding prior to the activation of phonological form (see Section 1.1.2). Two distinct stages are proposed for structure building. In the initial stage, termed *functional encoding*, the lemmas which best match the conceptual representation in the message are retrieved and assigned to grammatical functions appropriate for the thematic structure (e.g., agent → subject, patient → object, for a transitive active sentence such as 'Anne saw Bill'). Following function assignment, an appropriate phrase structure is generated to which the lemmas are attached. The process for generating phrase structure was elaborated in a model proposed by Pickering and Branigan (1998), which also incorporated links from lemma representations to nodes specifying the possible phrase structures in which they can occur. These 'combinatorial nodes' were initially linked only to verbs and encoded subcategorisation information. Later versions of the model extended the approach to nouns (Cleland & Pickering, 2003, 2006). Following function assignment, the selection of phrase structures in the model is driven by activation spreading from the lemmas with the most highly activated combinatorial node being selected (*constituent assembly*). Due to the direct links between lemmas and syntactic structures, this approach provides a clear mechanism through which lexical and syntactic representations can interact to determine the structure of the sentence produced.

Another approach which encodes explicit links between lemmas and syntactic structures employs tree-adjoining grammar (TAG; Ferreira, 2000; Frank, 2002; Momma, 2021, 2022). Momma (2021, 2022) proposes a TAG-based grammatical encoding model in which the syntactic structure for an utterance is constructed based on elementary trees. Elementary trees are complex structures headed by clause-taking verbs comprising a hierarchical syntactic structure with open nodes for constituents. For example, the elementary tree for a transitive verb like 'chase' would have two determiner phrase nodes for the sentence subject and object. More complex structures are created in the model by combining elementary trees either by a process of substitution or adjoining. In substitution, open nodes in an elementary tree are filled by appropriate tree structures; for example, an open determiner phrase node could be filled by a determiner phrase tree 'the girl'. The process of adjoining fills nodes with auxiliary trees containing recursive elements like adverbs and adjectives. In this model, lemmas are represented at a sub-tree level and are connected to the appropriate nodes of an elementary tree. The sub-tree level also contains nodes representing functional heads for structural options, such as DO and PO datives, which can be activated by thematic representations. Inhibitory links between sub-trees allow for a competitive lemma selection process. In contrast, elementary trees do not compete for selection. Elementary trees are stored in long-term memory and activated by the conceptual structure, either directly or via the conceptual activation of their sub-tree representations.

Momma (2021) proposed the model to explain the grammatical encoding of long-distance syntactic dependencies, such as the cross-clausal filler-gap dependency in the sentence 'Who do you think that the girl likes?'. This sentence has a syntactic dependency between the words 'who' (the filler) and 'likes' (the gap – i.e., the missing object for the verb). According to the model, speakers plan the structural dependency between such elements prior to planning the intervening material. Critically, elementary trees must encode all syntactic dependencies, including long-distance dependencies, within a phrase. Therefore, a minimal elementary tree for the sentence above must represent the cross-clausal filler-gap dependency. This elementary tree is abstract in that it represents critical grammatical information about the syntactic nature of the gap and the clause structure in which it occurs. However, it does not represent the material intervening between the filler and the gap. This is represented in a separate tree, and the process of tree adjoining enables this material to be inserted into the elementary tree at a later point during grammatical encoding. This model therefore encodes explicit links between lexical and syntactic representations, allowing them to interact during grammatical encoding.

In contrast, interactions between lemmas and syntactic structures are not a feature of a series of computational learning models of grammatical encoding (Chang, 2002; Chang et al., 2006; Dell & Chang, 2014). The Dual Path approach adopted in these models hinges on a strict separation between lexical retrieval and structure building. Similar to the lexically driven models described in Section 1.1.3, grammatical encoding is initiated following the construction of a conceptual message in which lexical concepts are bound to thematic roles and appropriate lemmas are activated by these lexical concepts. The models diverge, however, in that there is no process of function assignment in the Dual Path approach. Instead, the order of activation of lemmas is determined by the activation level of their lexical concepts, which is in turn determined by the weighting of their associated thematic roles. For example, during the production of an active sentence, the agent role would be most highly activated, while for passive sentences the patient role would have the highest activation level. Importantly, the activation of a lemma would be blind to the thematic role assignment of the associated lexical concept.

Syntactic structure is built by a sequencing system modelled as a simple recurrent network (SRN). This network has access only to the event semantics in the thematic structure and is blind to the lexical concepts. It learns syntactic categories and relationships between words through trial and error by predicting word order during training. The SRN stores the links between thematic structures and word orders via a layer of hidden units. During grammatical encoding, the most appropriate word order to convey the information encoded in a message is determined by the weighted thematic structure and the learned syntactic relationships in the SRN. The Dual Path model therefore explains grammatical encoding in terms of a predictive learning process operating as we comprehend speech, actively predicting the next word we will hear and learning from our mistakes (error-driven learning). It therefore provides an explicit mechanism for the acquisition of syntax (e.g., Fitz & Chang, 2017). Critically this approach allows no interaction between lexical information and structure building during grammatical encoding.

A competing alternative is Reitter, Keller and Moore's (2011) lexical model of priming. This model based on Adaptive Control of Thought—Rational (ACT-R) accounts for both short-term and long-term structural priming, and views both as a consequence of lexical priming. The model implements Combinatory Categorial Grammar (Steedman, 2000), where words are bound to subcategorisation information. It includes a declarative memory element with chunks of lexical information connected to chunks of syntactic information and a procedural memory element with if-then rules. Production occurs by sequential activation and retrieval of individual lexical and syntactic chunks from declarative memory; priming occurs because words are kept in a short-term buffer (the 'working memory' of the model) and are more likely to be reactivated, with their associated syntactic details, if they have been used recently. The spread of activation in the model explains lexically supported short-term priming as well as cumulative priming.

Finally, other approaches allow both lexical and structural representations to guide grammatical encoding (or, more specifically, linearisation). Theories of sentence planning are particularly well-suited to addressing questions about the degree of lexical and structural control of production because they make specific predictions about the type of information that *starts* or *triggers* production of a sentence. A well-known property of the language system is that it allows production to unfold incrementally: speakers plan utterances in small increments rather than in proposition-like units. So, when producing a novel utterance, what information do speakers tend to encode *first*? The precise nature of the incremental build-up of an utterance is described by two accounts – Linear Incrementality and Hierarchical Incrementality – which roughly follow from the assumptions of accounts proposing lexical and abstract syntactic control of production (see Figure 2). *Linearly incremental* planning assumes that utterances can be built up in word-like chunks. For example, the generation of a sentence can begin with the retrieval of a single word (corresponding to the concept that is mentioned first; e.g., either 'cowboy' or 'bull' in a sentence that will eventually be articulated as 'The cowboy caught the bull' or 'The bull was caught by the cowboy'). Activation of either noun commits the speaker to selection of either active or passive syntax (at least in English), which will result in the 'projection' of a syntactic structure to subsequently guide encoding of the remaining content words. The various word-sized planning units are joined together by basic sequencing rules (which are underspecified in this account). The attachment or joining of each new word-like unit to the previous one results in the emergence of a specific syntactic structure. In contrast,

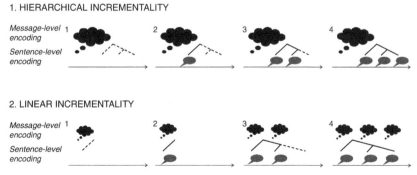

Figure 2 Schematic illustrating the relationship between message-level and sentence-level planning under the strong versions of (a) hierarchical incrementality and (b) lexical incrementality in the production of a transitive sentence with three content words in a sentence like 'The cowboy caught the bull' in four time steps (see Figure 3 for a paradigm eliciting such sentences).

Hierarchical Incrementality assumes that control of sentence planning and word sequencing lies in the hands of abstract structural processes responsible for generating a relational structure at the conceptual level and a corresponding syntactic structure at the linguistic level. Importantly, this structural framework is generated without lexical support: it precedes lexical retrieval and controls its timing, rather than being projected from a sequence of lexical retrieval operations (see e.g., Bock & Ferreira, 2014, for a review). In other words, speakers activate lexical items in the order in which the sentence syntax calls for them.

Hierarchical Incrementality is consistent with an elegant solution to the linearisation problem in production proposed by Dell and colleagues (2008; also see Momma, Buffinton, Slevc & Phillips, 2020). Dell and colleagues describe a model with a strict division of labour between semantics and syntax. Determining word order is the job of a syntactic 'traffic cop', or a mechanism consisting of a series of weights between syntactic sequential states and lexical items that enables speakers to 'say the right word at the right time'. The traffic cop tracks syntactic sequential states to ensure that only words of specific classes (e.g., determiners vs. nouns vs. verbs) are activated at specific points in time in the order required by the syntax of the developing sentence. Lexical retrieval is thus managed in an efficient manner by sequentially activating and deactivating lexical items that are semantically relevant and syntactically appropriate during production. For example, when producing the sentence 'The cowboy is catching the bull', the words 'cowboy' and 'catch' will not compete for the subject slot (but a suitable alternative word for referring to the agent, like 'man' or 'rancher', can). The division of labour is instantiated in the weights between syntax and the lexicon: content words have stronger links to semantics than to syntax, while function words have stronger links to syntax than to semantics. Momma and colleagues (2020) provided confirmatory experimental evidence that prime verbs and nouns with the same lexical form (e.g., 'is singing' vs. 'her singing') have different effects on production of semantically related verbs (e.g., 'whistling') in target sentences: prime verbs ('is singing') delay production of target verbs but prime nouns ('her singing') do not. Likewise, prime nouns delay production of target nouns, but prime verbs do not.

The strong versions of Linear and Hierarchical Incrementality described previously provide a useful reframing of the lexicalist versus abstract syntax debate. It is useful not only because it generates explicit testable predictions about control of production (as do other frameworks) but primarily because it does so at a level that provides fine-grained insight into production: adjudicating between these accounts requires tracking the time-course of production from message encoding until articulation, which allows for analysis of the coordination of multiple production processes. Importantly, it also provides a way of reconciling lexicalist and abstract syntax accounts. Determining the degree to which the production system supports one type of incremental planning over another by default – that is, the degree to which lexicalist and abstract syntax accounts provide a better description of the data – can lead to somewhat of a theoretical impasse. Instead, recent work in this area has suggested that there may be no default form of incrementality that is strictly determined by the architecture of the production system (e.g., Ferreira & Swets, 2002); instead, the production system may be flexible in supporting linear planning or hierarchical planning under different conditions (e.g., Konopka et al., 2018). Outlining the conditions under which planning is more likely to proceed in a linearly or hierarchically incremental fashion may ultimately lead to a more precise characterisation of grammatical encoding as being *primarily* lexically driven or *primarily* under the control of abstract syntax, but crucially, at present, this approach provides a new framework for explaining the complex processes through which language processes change and adapt to experience

The following sections of this Element describe empirical investigations into lexical and abstract syntactic control of grammatical encoding, first from the perspective of structural priming paradigms, which allow us to test what factors influence speakers' binary structure choices (Section 2), and then from the perspective of utterance planning paradigms, which allow us to test what factors influence grammatical encoding with finer-grained continuous temporal measures (Section 3).

2 The Independence of Syntactic and Lexical Representations: Evidence from Structural Priming

As described in Section 1.1.4, a key question in the field concerns the relationship between syntactic processes and other levels of representation during sentence production. Linguistic structure may emerge epiphenomenally from other levels of representation, such as conceptual structure and activation of lexical items (as proposed by lexicalist or functional accounts of syntax) or may be governed by an abstract structure-building syntactic process (as proposed by abstract syntactic accounts). Questions of representation such as these can be addressed by tracking the production of sentences with specific structures under controlled lab conditions as well as in natural speech (Branigan, 2007; Branigan & Pickering, 2017; Mahowald, James, Futrell & Gibson, 2016; Pickering & Ferreira, 2008). In the lab, the structural priming paradigm has been a particularly fruitful tool in the psycholinguistic toolbox in addressing this question.

Priming is the well-established finding that cognitive processes become easier to execute or to deploy after recent exposure to a particular stimulus or recent experience deploying similar processes. Thus, in priming studies, speakers are (a) exposed to a linguistic stimulus with specific properties in a prime trial and (b) produce an utterance in a subsequent target trial where they must select one among two (or more) linguistic options. If target sentences repeat a property of the primes, this suggests similarity in the underlying representation of the repeated linguistic property. In structural priming studies, speakers hear or read a sentence with a specific structure in prime trials and then produce a new sentence in target trials. Repetition of structure in the target trial – in the absence of other similarities between the prime and target – is taken to indicate that a sufficiently abstract syntactic frame was generated during processing of the prime to transfer to a new (target) sentence. This logic is not without its critics: any experience-dependent change that occurs in a target trial (such as repetition of a structure) is subject to cognitive constraints and can shift production preferences in a highly malleable language system that influence future productions (e.g., target sentences can act as 'primes' for subsequent sentences). Nevertheless, the question of *when* structural priming occurs and what factors modulate the *magnitude* of priming can shed light on the nature of the underlying syntactic representations generated at the moment of speaking.

In a seminal paper, Bock (1986) reported repetition of dative and transitive structures in a spontaneous picture-description task. Hearing and repeating a sentence with a prepositional-object (PO) dative structure in a prime trial (e.g., 'The wealthy widow gave the Mercedes to the church') increased the likelihood of speakers producing a prepositional dative in the subsequent target trial ('The man is reading a story to the boy'); likewise, hearing and repeating a sentence with a double-object (DO) dative structure in a prime trial (e.g., 'The wealthy widow gave the church the Mercedes') increased the likelihood of speakers producing a double-object dative structure in the subsequent target trial ('The man is reading the boy a story'). Analogous effects were obtained with active and passive sentences. Repetition of structure across unrelated sentences provided some of the first empirical evidence in favour of abstract syntax: neither meaning overlap nor lexical overlap were necessary to obtain repetition of syntactic structure, suggesting a syntactic locus for the repetition of structure and thus the involvement of abstract structural processes in the generation of simple sentences. This and further research focused on the question of whether repetition of structure is fundamentally syntactic in nature or whether similarity at other levels of representation (e.g., meaning and sound) changes the likelihood and magnitude of structural priming. Isolating effects due to abstract syntax is not a trivial problem, largely due to the difficulty in meeting the key experimental requirement – that is, unambiguously separating the contribution of syntactic and non-syntactic factors to linguistic structure.

2.1 Independence of Syntax from Meaning

In its earliest days, priming research addressed the question of independence of syntactic representations from meaning. There is an unavoidable parallelism between conceptual structure (or event structure) and syntactic structure: similar ideas are conveyed with similar word orders and underlying structures. The degree to which this parallelism is responsible for the development of a syntactic structure is a fundamental challenge for any account of abstract syntax. Specifically, when speakers reuse a particular structure, they may be doing this because of (a) similarities in conceptual structure across sentences that map onto similar syntactic structures, (b) facilitation of an independent abstract structural process, or (c) both (also see Prat-Sala & Branigan, 2000, for a discussion of the influence of discourse on structure choice). A crucial question then is whether some repetition of meaning is *necessary* for structural repetition to occur or whether meaning and syntax make *independent* contributions to the generation of sentence structure.

In support of the abstract syntax account, Bock and Loebell (1990) showed that repetition of structure across sentences can occur without any overlap in thematic roles (or event roles). Prepositional locatives (e.g., 1a) were found to be as effective as prepositional-object datives (1b) in priming production of target sentences with prepositional-dative syntax (1c, Experiment 1), despite differences in the thematic roles of the individual constituents in locative and dative sentences. Likewise, intransitive by-locative prime sentences (e.g., 2a) were as effective as passive prime sentences (2b) in priming production of target sentences with passive syntax (2c, Experiment 2), again despite differences in thematic roles of the individual constituents in intransitive and transitive sentences. Finally, sentences with superficially similar word orders and metric structures but different constituent structures did not show priming: prime sentences with prepositional-object dative syntax like 3a increased production of new prepositional-object datives (3c), but prime sentences with infinitive verbs like 3b did not (Experiment 3). These results were interpreted as strong evidence that the structures that generalised across sentences were syntactic in nature: what was required for priming to occur was similarity in constituent structure and not similarity in meaning or thematic arguments.

1. a. The wealthy widow drove the Mercedes to the church (prepositional locative)
   b. The wealthy widow gave the Mercedes to the church (prepositional dative)
   c. The boy is giving the apple to the teacher (prepositional dative)

2. a. The 747 was landing by the airport's control tower (by-locative)

    b. The 747 was alerted by the airport's control tower (by-passive)

    c. The man was stung by a bee (by-passive)

3. a. Susan brought a book to Stella (prepositional dative)

    b. Susan brought a book to study (infinitive)

    c. The boy is giving the apple to the teacher (prepositional dative)

Messenger, Branigan, McLean and Sorace (2012) tested a similar hypothesis for adults' and children's production of actives and passives, and showed that production of agent-patient passives increased after passive primes with three different thematic arguments, determined by the main sentence verb: agent-patient verbs (e.g., 4a), theme-experiencer verbs (e.g., 4b) and experiencer-theme verbs (e.g., 4c). In other words, speakers showed generalisation of a syntactic structure irrespective of the degree of thematic overlap between primes and targets.

4. a. The girl$_{PATIENT}$ was pushed by the boy$_{AGENT}$ (agent-patient verb)

    b. The girl$_{EXPERIENCER}$ was scared by the boy$_{THEME}$ (theme-experiencer verb)

    c. The girl$_{THEME}$ was seen by the boy$_{EXPERIENCER}$ (experiencer-theme verb)

A number of other findings are broadly consistent with a meaning-free account of structural repetition. For example, priming is observed across sentences with verb phrases that have similar syntax but different compositional meanings (idiomatic phrasal verbs like 'to pull off a robbery' and non-idiomatic phrasal verbs like 'to pull off a sweatshirt'; Konopka & Bock, 2009), suggesting that an analysis of word or phrase meanings is not part of the processes responsible for generating syntactic structures (but see Ziegler et al., 2018). Structural priming also occurs from prime sentences with novel verbs and anomalous verbs (Ivanova, Pickering, Branigan, McLean & Costa, 2012), as well as from sentences with missing verbs (Ivanova, Branigan, McLean, Costa & Pickering, 2017) and in artificial languages (Fehér, Wonnacott & Smith, 2016), which again suggests that repetition of structure is not sensitive to sentence or verb meaning. Finally, the complexity of individual constituent phrases (e.g., simple NPs vs. complex NPs) or the degree of match in phrasal complexity between primes and targets does not change the magnitude of priming, indicating that what matters for structural repetition is similarity in global rather than local syntactic structure across sentences (Hardy, Wheeldon & Segaert, 2020).

In fact, such repetition effects may not be unique to language. Repetition of abstract structure has also been observed across cognitive domains – from simple arithmetic to relative clause attachment in language. For example, solving arithmetic problems with internal structures analogous to high-attachment and low-attachment sentences increases production of high-attachment and low-attachment sentence fragment continuations, respectively (Scheepers et al., 2011; also see Scheepers & Sturt, 2014). Similar attachment priming effects have also been observed from music sequences and action descriptions to relative clause attachment in language (Van de Cavey & Hartsuiker, 2016). Finding that sequences with similar hierarchical structures in one domain can prime analogous structures in the linguistic domain argues for the existence of a highly abstract and domain-general structural processor (also see Whittlesea & Wright, 1997).

At the same time, there is evidence of similarity in event structure across linguistic primes and targets influencing structure choice. Two non-syntactic variables that have received considerable attention are effects of referent animacy as well as thematic role, event structure and semantic similarity on structure choice.

Animacy. The first testcase for abstract syntax theories is the role of animacy in determining word order. Speakers display a strong cross-linguistic bias to assign agents to syntactically prominent positions and/or sentence-initial positions, suggesting a clear influence of conceptual representations and conceptual accessibility on sentence structure. The genesis of this effect may be in a general bias to prioritise detecting agency and causality in linguistic and non-linguistic cognition (Wilson, Zuberbühler & Bickel, 2022). To determine the extent of animacy effects on structure choice, studies have pitted the effects of referent animacy (e.g., agent and patient animacy) and syntactic priming on structure choice against one another. The persistence of structure together with persistence of a mapping of an animate or inanimate referent to a particular grammatical function (*concept-to-function* mapping) or to a particular linear position (*concept-to-linear order* mapping) would indicate a strong link between conceptual representations and grammatical processes. Bock (1986) reported numeric trends suggesting that animacy can indeed restrict structural priming. However, Bock, Loebell and Morey (1992) showed that syntactic priming occurred over and above any effects of character animacy on structure choice (also see Ziegler & Snedeker, 2018, in this section), suggesting that syntactic structure can be manipulated independently of the bias to assign animate entities to specific linear sentence positions. Evidence of additivity (rather than interactivity) of animacy effects and structural priming effects on structure choice suggest that the two effects may have a different locus.

Finer-grained investigation of animacy effects on production have much to gain from cross-linguistic research, particularly with languages that permit more variation in word order than English (e.g., Mandarin Chinese in Cai, Pickering & Branigan, 2012; Odawa in Christianson & Ferreira, 2005; Japanese in Tanaka, Branigan, McLean & Pickering, 2011; see Branigan, 2007 and Norcliffe & Konopka, 2015 for reviews). At issue is the question of whether highly accessible animate referents are assigned to privileged syntactic roles (e.g., the subject role; *concept-to-function* mapping) or whether they are simply encoded early and assigned to sentence-initial positions (*concept-to-linear order* mapping). In English, subjecthood is confounded with linear word order. In languages with fewer constraints on linear word order, the two can be dissociated (if, for example, the grammar allows subjects to not be produced sentence initially). Cai and colleagues (2012) pitted the *concept-to-function* and *concept-to-linear order* hypotheses against each other in a priming task with speakers of Mandarin Chinese, which has a more flexible word order for dative sentences (e.g., it allows direct objects of dative sentences like 'The cowboy gave the sailor the book' to be topicalised). The results showed persistence in the assignment of concepts to the same grammatical functions (e.g., themes as direct objects) as well as in the assignment of concepts to the same linear positions (e.g., themes before verbs), which supports an account in which mappings from concepts to functions and to linear order can occur in parallel.

Thematic roles. Evidence that is more problematic for the abstract syntax account comes from studies assessing repetition of thematic role order pitted against repetition of structure. Notably, structural processing choice *is* sensitive to thematic role order. Chang, Bock and Goldberg (2003) showed priming of theme-location/location-theme role orders across prime and target sentences where the surface syntactic structure was held constant: sentences with theme-location order like 5a primed theme-location order in new sentences like 5c more than sentences with location-theme order like 5b (also see Hare & Goldberg, 2000 and Ziegler & Snedeker, 2018). This finding suggests that the order of thematic roles (or thematic role mappings) is a relevant feature during the mapping of conceptual representations onto linguistic structures (also see Chang et al., 2006).

5. a. The maid rubbed polish onto the table (theme-location order)

   b. The maid rubbed the table with polish (location-theme order)

   c. The farmer heaped straw onto the wagon (theme-location order)

Ziegler and Snedeker (2018) tested how similarity in thematic role order influenced priming with a finer-grained manipulation. They compared priming between sentences with the same surface syntactic structures but differences in thematic roles: datives and locatives both have themes and goals, but more specifically, the goals are *recipients* in dative sentences (6a, 6b) and *destinations* in locative sentences (6c, 6d). They showed dative-to-dative priming as well as locative-to-locative priming (i.e., sentences with the same thematic roles), as expected, but no locative-to-dative and dative-to-locative priming (i.e., sentences with different thematic roles), unless locatives had animate goals (6e, 6f) so that animacy features in datives and locatives matched. Thus, across a series of experiments, the results suggested a gradient of syntactic priming effects, such that the magnitude of priming increased with increasing overlap in animacy and thematic role order in primes and targets.

6. a. The boy hands the *suitcase* to his *mother* (PO dative: *theme* + *goal*[recipient])

    b. The boy hands his *mother* the *suitcase* (DO dative: *goal*[recipient] + *theme*)

    c. The boy loads the *bag* on the *cart* (theme-first locative: *theme* + inanimate *goal* [destination])

    d. The boy loads the *cart* with the *bag* (theme-second locative: inanimate *goal* [destination] + theme)

    e. The boy sprayed cologne on the man (theme-first locative: theme + animate *goal* [destination])

    f. The boy sprayed the man with cologne (theme-second locative: animate *goal* [destination] + theme)

Perhaps the most interesting counter-argument to abstract syntactic accounts is Ziegler, Bencini, Goldberg and Snedeker's (2019) evaluation of Bock's (1986) by-locative priming. Ziegler and colleagues used a prime-target paradigm with written primes followed by presentation of target pictures that elicited active and passive descriptions. Their study replicated by-passive and by-locative priming of by-passives (7a and 7b primed 7d) but showed that this effect did not generalise to near-locatives primes (7c did not prime 7d), suggesting a role for lexical repetition in eliciting repetition of structure and calling for a re-examination of the evidence in Bock (1986) used to argue for abstract syntax.

7. a. The 747 was radioed by the airport control tower (passive)

    b. The 747 was landing by the airport control tower (*by*-locative)

    c. The 747 was landed near the airport control tower (*near*-locative)

    d. The boy was hit by the ball (passive)

Semantic and event structure similarity. Finally, exposure to sentences with similar semantic information, expressed via individual content words rather than at the level of event structure, also influences structure selection. For example, Cleland and Pickering (2003) showed enhanced noun-phrase priming with semantically related referents: speakers were more likely to produce target descriptions like 'the sheep that's red' after exposure to primes with semantically related nouns (like 'the goat that's red') than unrelated nouns (like 'the book that's red'; a *semantic boost*). Likewise, Konopka and Kuchinsky (2015) found enhanced priming of actives and passives when primes and targets had conceptually related verbs (e.g., 'tripping' and 'pushing') than when they had unrelated verbs ('paying' and 'pushing'; also see Bernolet, Colleman & Hartsuiker, 2014, for evidence of a *sense boost*, and Gruberg, Ostran, Momma & Ferreira, 2019, for persistence of structure in repeated events). More dramatically, Bunger, Papafragou and Trueswell (2013) found that, when describing motion events (e.g., an alien driving into a cave), participants were more likely to mention path information in target sentences when primes also mentioned path information, both when using the same and different verbs. This priming of the content of preverbal messages suggests that priming of structure may extend to priming of event representations (also see Bernolet, Hartsuiker & Pickering, 2009 and Ziegler et al., 2018).

In sum, recent work in this area shows evidence of both event semantics and abstract syntax influencing speakers' structure choice. Importantly, this evidence is not incompatible with accounts of abstract syntax as repetition of meaning does not uniquely account for speakers' structure choices. What is crucial for abstract syntax accounts is that syntactic structures are not purely 'limnings of meaning' (Bock & Loebell, 1990; Chang et al., 2006): with the exception of Ziegler and colleagues (2019), repetition of structure has been shown to occur across sentences *in spite of* differences in event semantics.

2.2 Independence of Syntax from the Lexicon

A second key question in assessing the independence of syntax from other levels of representation is that of lexical contributions to syntax. Language production requires rapid activation and integration of words and structures to construct grammatically correct utterances with context-appropriate lexical content. Interactions between lexical items and grammar are thus a natural component of this integration process. In structural priming, the question of lexical influences on structure has been one of the most active areas addressing the debate between lexicalist and abstract syntactic theories of structure over the decades. The initial evidence provided by Bock (1986, 1989) was that priming occurs without similarity in meaning across prime and target sentences but also without repetition of either content words or function words. Thirty years later, there is ample evidence of lexical involvement in structure building but also development of models reconciling this evidence with abstract accounts of syntax.

2.2.1 The Lexical Boost in Structural Priming

Repetition of meaning normally entails repetition of lexical items. Thus, as with repetition of event semantics, one might expect to see evidence for the involvement of the lexicon in speakers' structural choices in the form of a lexical boost in structural priming. Indeed, using a sentence completion task, Pickering and Branigan (1998) showed that speakers were more likely to repeat the syntax of a prime PO (or DO sentence) in a new target sentence when primes and targets used the same verb (8a, 8b) than when they did not (8c, 8d).

8. a. The racing driver showed the torn overall ... (prime sentence biased towards PO completion)
   b. The patient showed ... (to-be-completed target sentence)
   c. The racing driver gave the torn overall ... (prime sentence biased towards PO completion)
   d. The patient showed ... (to-be-completed target sentence)

Since then, this *lexical boost* (or lexical enhancement of priming) has been replicated in numerous studies with a range of sentence elicitation paradigms and in corpora (Gries, 2005), and with repetition of both verbs and nouns (Cleland & Pickering, 2003). Pickering and Branigan's (1998) proposed representation basis of lexical influences on structure choice focuses on activation at the lemma level. On their account, lemma nodes are linked to combinatorial nodes, which specify what structures a verb can be used in (e.g., *give* can be used in both prepositional-object and double-object dative structures, while *donate* can only be used with propositional-object syntax). This information is activated during processing of a prime sentence. Residual activation of combinatorial nodes can bias structure selection in a subsequent target trial in favour of the recently activated structure. Importantly, the link between a combinatorial node and the verb lemma also remains temporarily activated, so repetition of the same verb from prime to target increases the likelihood of selecting a recently used structure beyond the level supported by activation of combinatorial nodes alone. The magnitude of this lexical enhancement of priming is noteworthy: the odds of repetition of structure double in sentences with than without lexical overlap (Mahowald et al., 2016).

It is not clear from Pickering and Branigan's account (1998) whether the lexical boost is a conflation of two effects: a *semantic boost* driven by repetition of meaning plus a *lexical boost* due only to repeated activation of the same lexical information. Santesteban, Pickering and McLean (2010) provided evidence that distinguished between these possibilities by testing whether lexical similarity without semantic overlap can modulate structural priming. Their experiments compared structural priming of NPs (e.g., 'the red bat' vs. 'the bat that's red') with non-homophonous and homophonous nouns. Priming was equally strong from primes with nouns that repeated meaning and sound information (e.g., the animal *bat* in primes and targets) and homophonous nouns that repeated sound information alone (the animal *bat* and a cricket *bat* in primes and targets, respectively; but see Cleland & Pickering, 2003). This *homophone boost* suggests that overlap at the word-form level is sufficient to observe enhanced priming (also see Konopka & Bock, 2009, for evidence of a lexical boost in sentences with idiomatic verbs that repeat word forms but not meaning).

A number of findings regarding the involvement of the lexicon in structure building are important for keeping these effects in perspective. The first observation is that structural priming is boosted by – but not determined by – lexical repetition: the lexical boost is an enhancement of structural repetition rather than a precondition for structural repetition to occur. Observing lexically unsupported priming is indeed treated as the golden standard for classifying repetition of structure as 'syntactic' in nature (e.g., Fehér et al., 2016). This definition places key constraints on lexical accounts of syntax and requires clarification of how potential links between lexical items and syntax modulate structure choice.

For example, not all lexical repetition results in a lexical boost. Repetition is mediated by the syntactic role of the repeated words: a lexical boost has been observed with repetition of open-class words that are syntactic heads (Carminati, van Gompel & Wakeford, 2019; Ivanova et al., 2017; van Gompel, Wakeford & Kantola, 2022) but not syntactic non-heads. Repetition of closed-class words such as *to* and *for* in dative sentences (Bock, 1989), or *by* in locatives and passives (Bock & Loebell, 1990) does not create a lexical boost (but see Ziegler et al., 2018). Further, lexical similarity alone is also not sufficient for repetition. For example, Ferreira (2003) used a sentence-recall production task to demonstrate that the use of the optional complementiser 'that' in sentences such as 9d could only be primed by sentences that included a complementiser 'that' (i.e., the same lexical item playing a similar syntactic role, 9a) but not by a determiner 'that' (i.e., the same lexical item playing a different syntactic role, 9b) or a noun-complement 'that' (i.e., the same lexical item in a different syntactic context, 9c). Importantly, both the inclusion and exclusion of the complementiser 'that' could be primed – a finding consistent with a structural rather than lexical locus for priming effect.

9. a. The company ensured that the farm was covered for two million dollars

    b. The company insured that farm for two million dollars

    c. The theory that penguins built the igloo was completely false

    d. The mechanic mentioned (that) the antique car could use a tune-up

Momma (2022) built on these findings by demonstrating that the priming of complementiser 'that' can be lexically boosted by the repetition of verbs biased for its use (e.g., Bernolet & Hartsuiker, 2010). This boost was observed when both prime and target either did or did not feature cross-clausal filler-gap dependencies (10a and 10b, respectively). However, when the prime sentence (but not the target) contained a cross-clausal filler-gap dependency (e.g., 10a), the lexical boost disappeared.

10. a. Who did the manager imply (that) he would promote?

    b. The manager implied (that) he would promote the employee

This result is problematic due to the explicit memory account of the lexical boost, which would predict that a boost should be observed in all conditions. Momma (2022) proposed that lexically independent structural priming is the result of an enhanced link between a concept and a node of an elementary tree, whereas lexical boost effects are due to the residual activation of elementary trees (similar to the priming mechanisms proposed by Pickering & Branigan, 1998). Critically, according to the TAG model, elementary trees must contain all syntactic dependencies as well as complementiser features. Therefore, the sentences in 10 will be represented by different elementary trees which are headed by the same verb.

Second, repetition of structure across sentences with and without overlap in content words has a different time-course. Lexical and abstract syntactic accounts make different predictions about the duration of structural priming effects, following directly from differences in their mechanistic explanations of priming. Activation-based accounts, such as Pickering and Branigan's (1998) lexical account, predict short-lived priming: by definition, activation dissipates quickly, so any activation of links between verb nodes and combinatorial nodes that produces a lexical boost in the short term may fail to produce a lexical boost in the long term. Accounts that emphasise a syntactic locus of structural repetition predict persistence of lexically *un*supported priming.

Consistent with abstract accounts, structural priming has been observed across different lags within the same experiment (Bernolet, Collina & Hartsuiker, 2016; Bock & Griffin, 2000; Bock, Dell, Chang & Onishi, 2007; Hartsuiker et al., 2008; Kaschak & Borreggine, 2008; Kaschak, Loney & Borreggine, 2006), across different sessions of the same experiment (Kaschak, Kutta & Schatschneider, 2011), and in natural speech (Gries, 2005) in sentences without lexical overlap (see Figure 3 for an example of Lag 0 and Lag 2 priming). Priming effects are also obtained regardless of the cover task given to participants (i.e., regardless of whether participants'

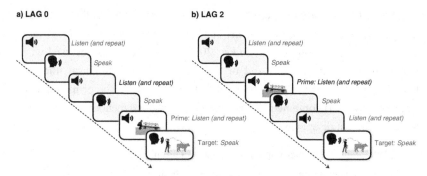

Figure 3 Schematic illustrating a prime-target structural priming paradigm in (a) lag 0 with adjacent prime and target trials (white cells), and in (b) lag 2 with the prime and target separated by two intervening filler trials (grey cells). Recorded prime sentences with active or passive syntax: 'The man is lifting the bench' / 'The bench is being lifted by the man'. Target sentences eliciting active or passive sentences: 'The cowboy is catching the bull' / 'The bull is being caught by the cowboy'.

attention is directed to the sentence form or not; Bock et al., 1992) and remarkably even in participants with compromised episodic memory (anterograde amnesics; Ferreira, Bock, Wilson & Cohen, 2008; Heyselaar, Segaert, Walvoort, Kessels & Hagoort, 2017). In contrast, the lexical boost in syntactic priming declines when primes and targets are separated by as few as two intervening sentences (Hartsuiker, Bernolet, Schoonbaert, Speybroeck & Vanderelst, 2008; Kaschak & Borreggine, 2008; Konopka & Bock, 2005). For example, Hartsuiker and colleagues (2008) compared the magnitude of dative PO/DO priming at lags 0, 2, and 6, and showed a lexical boost only at lag 0. The sharp decline in lexically supported priming suggests that lexical contributions to structure repetition are short-lived.

A complementary approach showed that the magnitude of priming effects can vary with the extent of repeated exposure to alternative structures but not to repeated exposure with specific verbs. Kaschak and colleagues (2006) tested whether participants' sensitivity to a PO-DO priming manipulation was modulated by recent and repeated experience with the primed structures (i.e., a form of cumulative priming). In Experiment 1, after an exposure phase where the ratio of PO and DO sentences was manipulated (50:50 in the same block vs. 50:50 but in separate blocks vs. 100:0), priming was only observed in participants who had been exposed to both structures at the beginning of the study. Participants who had been exposed to only PO or only DO sentences (i.e., a 100:0 ratio of PO:DO structures or DO:PO structures) did not respond to the priming manipulation. In Experiment 2, sensitivity to the priming manipulation also varied in a graded fashion, in line with the strength of the structural bias introduced in the exposure phase (50:50 vs. 75:25 vs. 100:0). This effect was not replicated by Kaschak (2007), who proposed that the exposure phase shifts base rates for individual structures (with stronger shifts for the dispreferred PO structure) but not the magnitude of priming effects. Subsequently, Kaschak and Borreggine (2008) tested whether these biases are affected by verb repetition in the exposure phase and again showed structural repetition only in participants who had been exposed to both structural alternatives prior to the priming task. Crucially, these effects were not modulated by verb repetition or by the presentation of the verb in one or both structures. In other words, what mattered for structure choice was the frequency of use of individual structures rather than the frequency of use of individual structures with specific verbs.

Thus, testing the longevity of abstract syntactic priming and lexically supported priming shows a critical dissociation. On balance, the short-lived nature of the lexical boost – arguably the strongest evidence for involvement of the lexicon in structure building – and the persistence of abstract priming suggests that the two effects have a different source. These results favour a multifactorial account of priming, one where the binding of words to structures responsible for the lexical boost is dynamic and short-lived, while the persistence of structure choice long after the lexical boost has decayed arises from longer-term learning of structure-building procedures in an abstract syntactic system. Chang and colleagues (2006) account for this finding by proposing an implicit learning mechanism that predicts both short-term and longer-term repetition of structure and that is resistant to episodic forgetting, and speculate that a separate mechanism, relying on explicit memory, may explain lexical influences on structure choice (see Section 1.1.4; Chang, Janciauskas & Fitz, 2012).

The proposal of explicit memory retrieval explaining the lexical boost is important for clarifying the coordination of lexical and syntactic processes during grammatical encoding. If repetition of structure is driven by memory for the prime sentences, this makes the priming paradigm less suitable for addressing questions about the production architecture, such as the nature of the links between individual lexical items and structural information. For example, Scheepers, Raffray and Myachykov (2017) showed that repetition of any content word from PO/DO-primes to PO/DO targets can produce a lexical boost (agents, verbs, recipients, themes). In fact, the magnitude of priming increased with increasing overlap in content words, producing a *cumulative lexical boost* effect. Scheepers and colleagues proposed that repetition of lexical items serves as a powerful retrieval cue: quite simply, the more lexical repetition, the stronger the memory cues and the higher the likelihood of structural repetition. Bernolet and colleagues (2016) also suggested that explicit memory may contribute to structural repetition even when primes and target do not share lexical items, based on the finding that both structural priming and explicit memory for the prime sentences declined over lags (from Lag 0 to Lag 6) in their experiments. There was, however, evidence of cumulative lexically unsupported priming: speakers' production of target structures increased as a function of the number of these structures produced within an experimental session. In a more direct test of the memory hypothesis, Zhang, Bernolet and Hartsuiker (2020) showed that adding a cognitive load to the production task reduced structural priming effects in adjacent prime and target trials, both in sentences with and without lexical overlap (but see Yan, Martin & Slevc, 2018, for a different view). Further insight into the coordination of lexical and structural processes is provided by studies assessing verb biases and cumulative priming effects (Section 2.2.2).

2.2.2 Verb Bias and Structural Priming

Stronger evidence for the involvement of the lexicon in structure building comes from studies of verb bias. Among verbs that can appear in alternative syntactic structures (e.g., PO and DO datives), some demonstrate a strong bias for one structure over the other, while others show weaker biases or are considered to be equi-biased. These biases illustrate one of the main premises of lexicalist accounts of syntax, that is, the claim that lexical activation is a key driver of structure-building procedures, or that, put differently, syntax is 'projected' from the lexicon. For such biases to arise, the production system must keep track of individual verb-structure pairings over a speaker's lifetime (a form of *cumulative* priming) and store verb-specific frequency information that reflects the statistics of the input. This information is then activated when a known verb is used on a new occasion and can bias selection of the most frequent structural alternative for that verb.

In support of this lexical view, Melinger and Dobel (2005) showed that speakers' structure choices can be influenced by the presentation of a single verb. In prime trials in their study, participants read non-alternating dative verbs (i.e., verbs that were strongly biased towards either PO or DO dative structures), and then saw pictures meant to elicit dative descriptions in target trials. Target descriptions were consistent with the bias of prime verbs: speakers produced more PO descriptions after PO-biased verbs and more DO descriptions after DO-biased verbs. Thus, activation of a verb with strong structural biases out of a sentence context was sufficient to influence structure choice in line with these biases.

However, the mere existence of verb biases is seemingly in direct contrast with the observation that the lexical boost in priming declines over time (discussed in the previous section). How do results such as Melinger and Dobel's (2005) as well as Kaschak and Borreggine's (2008) square with the observation of a short-lived lexical boost in priming? Conversely, if verb-structure pairings are dynamic, as assumed by implicit accounts of priming, how do verb biases come about in the first place? The answer arguably lies in the difference between short-term priming effects and long-term (or cumulative) priming.

Studies assessing structural priming with biased verbs *in the short term* provide an explanation that is more compatible with implicit learning accounts than with lexicalist accounts of syntax. Bernolet and Hartsuiker (2010) tested how existing verb biases modulate the magnitude of dative PO/DO structural priming in a full-sentence prime-target paradigm and showed an important difference between baseline structural preferences and sensitivity to priming of different verbs. Production of target sentences in a baseline condition showed strong effects of verb bias: participants generated more sentences with PO syntax than DO syntax, consistent with the biases of the verbs used in these sentences. At the same time, structure choice was also modulated by the priming manipulation: more PO/DO sentences were produced after PO/DO-primes. Importantly, participants' productions showed an inverse priming effect: priming from DO-primes (i.e., primes with dispreferred DO syntax) was stronger than priming from PO-primes (i.e., primes with preferred PO syntax; see Segaert, Weber, Cladder-Micus & Hagoort, 2014, for a similar effect with active and passive structures). This effect was further modulated by the individual 'bias scores' of both prime and target verbs: DO-primes had the strongest effect on target sentences when they featured PO-biased verbs, and target sentences with PO-biased verbs showed the strongest effects of DO-primes. In other words, the verb-structure combinations that are encountered less frequently produced the strongest priming.

The results are consistent with a key prediction of the implicit learning account of structural priming (Bock & Griffin, 2000; Chang et al., 2006; Jaeger & Snider, 2013), namely the fact that encountering a surprising structure in a prime trial results in stronger error-based learning and thus increases the likelihood of producing a dispreferred structure in a target trial. This account also explains why dispreferred structures continue to exist in speakers' linguistic repertoire: these structures receive a large boost with each use, which effectively ensures that they do not prime themselves out of existence (Ferreira & Bock, 2006).

In contrast, studies assessing structural priming with biased verbs *in the long term* show that verb biases do persist. Coyle and Kaschak (2008) proposed that repeated exposure to verbs in the same structures (i.e., using a manipulation meant to simulate specific verb biases) *can* produce longer-lasting, lexically enhanced structural priming, and that these effects can be observed in production tasks with a minor modification. Namely, Coyle and Kaschak hypothesised that any longer-lasting effects induced in the exposure phase of their experiment may not be visible in the priming phase because prime trials exert a strong and immediate influence on structure choice on target trials, but should be observable in the same target trials when not preceded by primes. Indeed, examining structure choice in target trials after an exposure phase meant to induce specific verb biases showed the persistence of these biases. Thus, the rapid decay of the lexical boost in priming studies need not imply that lexical contributions to structure repetition are short-lived: verb biases may come about due to repeated exposure to specific verb-structure bindings on a time scale that exceeds that of most priming studies in the lab.

2.2.3 Structural Priming in Bilinguals

As a field, psycholinguistics initially favoured research on language processing in monolingual populations. Studies on bilingual language processing, however, are now plentiful. Much like cross-linguistic research, bilingualism provides new opportunities for establishing the nature of processing similarities across languages or constraints on processing (also see Blasi, Henrich, Adamou, Kemmerer & Majid, 2022, for a discussion of the need to broaden the field's scope of research to languages other than English). In particular, by testing whether syntactic structures can generalise from one language to another, bilingual studies contribute valuable evidence to the debate about the balance of lexical and structural influences in grammatical encoding (Hartsuiker & Pickering, 2008).

Early research in this area showed lexically unsupported repetition of structure in bilinguals that closely mirrored findings from monolingual speakers (Loebell & Bock, 2003): priming occurred between English and German dative sentences (both languages allow PO and DO syntax) but not between English and German transitive sentences (English and German passive syntax differs). Later studies showed reliable between-language priming even across languages with different word orders (e.g., Bernolet et al., 2009; Hwang & Shin, 2019; also see Khoe, Tsoukala, Kootstra & Frank, 2021, for a model). These results are strongly supportive of abstract syntactic accounts in demonstrating that syntactic structure can persist in the absence of *any* lexical similarity between prime and target sentences, as long as there was syntactic similarity in the prime and target sentences (Bernolet et al., 2007). Based on similar evidence with English and Spanish transitive sentences, Hartsuiker, Pickering and Veltkamp (2004) proposed a shared-syntax model that extended Pickering and Branigan's (1998) lexical account of priming by adding combinatorial nodes linked to lemmas in two languages rather than only one language. However, bilinguals and language learners do show sensitivity to structure frequencies (i.e., stronger priming for less frequent structures; Hwang & Shin, 2019; Kaan & Chun, 2018; Kootstra & Doedens, 2016), which is more consistent with implicit learning accounts.

As in research on monolingual production, further studies considered the extent of lexical involvement in structural processing and showed a high degree of similarity in within-language and between-language priming. Most strikingly, Salamoura and Williams (2006) found evidence of single-verb priming comparable to Melinger and Dobel (2005) in bilingual speakers: presenting PO-only and DO-only verb primes in one language (L1, Dutch) increased production of PO and DO target sentences, respectively, in a second language (L2, English). Schoonbaert, Hartsuiker and Pickering (2007) showed that priming PO and DO syntax from L1 to L2 was enhanced when primes and targets shared the same verb (irrespective of the verb's cognate status), although the cross-linguistic *translation-equivalent* boost was smaller than the within-language lexical boost. An analogous *translation-equivalent* boost was not observed from L2 to L1, which can be explained by differences in the ease with which L1 and L2 verbs activate each other (L1 targets may not reactivate L2 primes as strongly as L2 targets reactivate L1 primes). Cross-linguistic priming of NP structure (e.g., *the girl's apple* vs. *the apple of the girl*; Bernolet, Hartsuiker & Pickering, 2012) did show a cognate effect, suggesting a possible role for feedback from phonology to the lemma level in line with interactive models of lexical access (but see Cai et al., 2012, for a different argument). However, the longevity of the *translation-equivalent boost* – that is, the key parameter supporting interpretations of structural repetition in terms of implicit learning of abstract structures rather than in terms of lexicalist accounts in monolingual speakers – remains to be determined (see van Gompel & Arai, 2018, for a review).

These results are broadly compatible with accounts assuming shared syntactic representations across languages, as well as some degree of dependence on lexical information. Importantly, the fact that proficiency levels vary across speakers as well as within speakers over time offers a unique means of determining how the balance between lexically unsupported and lexically supported syntactic processing might shift with linguistic experience (Hartsuiker & Bernolet, 2017; see Jackson, 2018, for a review). For example, the magnitude of cross-linguistic priming without lexical repetition was found to increase with speakers' proficiency in the target (L2) language but the magnitude of priming *with lexical support* was larger in speakers with lower L2 proficiency (Bernolet, Hartsuiker & Pickering, 2013; also see Jackson & Ruf, 2017). This suggests greater overlap in L1 and L2 structural processes in more proficient speakers but more reliance on the lexicon (i.e., less abstraction of syntax) in less proficient speakers. Such results are consistent with early descriptions of developmental changes in children (see e.g., Tomasello, 2000, for arguments about lexical dependence; Fisher, 2002, for arguments about abstract syntax; Rowland et al., 2012 and Peter, Chang, Pine, Blything & Rowland, 2015, for an updated account).

2.2.4 Structural Priming in Dialogue

Going beyond lexicalist and abstract syntactic accounts, psycholinguistic theories have also suggested that repetition of structure, together with repetition of a number of linguistic properties, may serve a communicative function in dialogue (Ferreira & Bock, 2006; Pickering & Garrod, 2004). Interlocutors normally establish common ground and align representations over the course of a conversation. Alignment at the semantic and lexical level in conversational settings is well-established: for example, speakers repeat lexical items previously used in the discourse (Levelt & Kelter, 1982) and begin to refer to known referents with reduced lexical descriptions ('the dancer' instead of a longer description for a tangram resembling a cartoon person in motion; Clark & Wilkes-Gibbs, 1986). They also reliably produce target sentences that repeat structures recently used by conversational partners in prime sentences (datives and NPs in collaborative card-matching tasks; Branigan, Pickering & Cleland, 2000; Branigan, Pickering, McLean & Cleland, 2007; Cleland & Pickering, 2003), both within and across languages (Hartsuiker & Pickering, 2008). Such findings have a number of implications.

First, the occurrence of structural repetition in dialogue shows that priming can occur from comprehension to production as readily as from production to production. Early priming studies that used non-interactive paradigms involved a production task in both prime and target trials: participants heard a prime sentence which they had to repeat out loud and then generated a new sentence in target trials (e.g., Bock, 1986). Repetition of a prime sentence implies that, in principle, any changes observed in target trials could be attributed to the engagement of production processes in prime trials, rather than showing generalisation directly from comprehension to production. More recent research has ruled out this explanation: in comprehension-to-production priming studies, participants are exposed to sentences with a given structure in a prime trial without immediately repeating them out loud, and production is then monitored in a subsequent target trial. Bock and colleagues (2007) reported structural priming effects of similar magnitude – and similar persistence across lags – to tasks requiring production of both primes and targets, suggesting that generalisation of structure is not compromised by changes in modality (repetition of prime sentences, however, may serve a more supportive function in second language production; see Jackson & Ruf, 2018).

By analogy to prime-target paradigms used in the lab, utterances produced by one conversational partner in a dialogue serve as 'comprehension primes' and utterances produced by the other conversational partner are 'production targets'. But does structural repetition in dialogue occur automatically or is dialogue 'special'? Communicative success is often described as a joint effort, prompting questions about modulation of priming by the social nature of the production setting: one might expect repetition effects to be larger in dialogue than in single-speaker, non-interactive settings (or rather, given that language use in interactive settings is the norm rather than the exception, one might expect repetition effects in non-interactive settings to underestimate the magnitude of repetition effects in everyday language use). This is indeed often the case. For example, Branigan and colleagues (2000, 2007) and Cleland and Pickering (2003) reported priming effects that were larger than in most non-interactive studies. Schoot, Hagoort and Segaert (2019) confirmed these differences in a between-participant comparison of priming in an interlocutor-present and interlocutor-absent condition, suggesting that repetition of structure may not simply occur automatically but rather that it may be additionally influenced by speakers' communicative goals. However, Ivanova, Horton, Swets, Kleinman and Ferreira (2020) obtained priming effects of similar magnitude in interlocutor-present and interlocutor-absent conditions, both with between-participant and within-participant manipulations, and argued that potential differences between interactive and non-interactive priming effects in earlier studies may be due to differences in participants' attention and engagement in the two types of settings. Consistent with this hypothesis is the observation of stronger priming in corpus data from a goal-driven task than in spontaneous conversation (Reitter & Moore, 2014).

If dialogue is special, one might also expect the magnitude of repetition effects to vary between two-party and multi-party settings together with participants' roles in the conversational exchanges. Speakers are indeed more likely to reuse recently heard structures when they are addressed directly by an interlocutor than when are were not addressed directly (i.e., when the prime sentence is addressed to another speaker in the conversational setting; Branigan et al., 2007), consistent with the hypothesis that repetition of structure may be mediated by heightened attention and task engagement. The magnitude of structural repetition can also vary with the identity and social evaluations of one's conversational partner (e.g., humans vs. computer-like avatars in Heyselaar, Hagoort & Segaert, 2017; likeable vs. less likeable confederates in Balcetis & Dale, 2005; teachers evaluated more vs. less positively in Hwang & Chun, 2018) as well as evaluations of the likelihood of communicative success (e.g., humans vs. computers in Branigan, Pickering, Pearson & McLean, 2010), although 'social' effects can also be observed in non-interactive paradigms (Weatherholtz, Campbell-Kibler & Jaeger, 2014). Interestingly, the magnitude of repetition does not seem to vary with the degree to which conversational partners align with the participants' productions (Schoot et al., 2019).

The larger question of whether structural alignment systematically supports communicative *success*, however, is still open. While communicative pressures can shape language structure (e.g., Christensen et al., 2016; Fehér et al., 2016), the evidence linking repetition of structure to communicative benefits is mixed. Structural alignment can reduce processing times in production and comprehension (e.g., Ferreira & Bock, 2006; Pickering & Garrod, 2004), but structural repetition effects need not be partner specific (e.g., Ferreira, Kleinman, Kraljic & Siu, 2012) and are not directly correlated with task success (e.g., Branigan et al., 2007; Ivanova et al., 2020). The scarcity of supporting evidence may be due to a number of factors. It is possible that repetition of structure alone is less clearly linked to communicative success than repetition of lexical items (i.e., lexical alignment, which is an explicit and strategic choice made by the speaker; e.g., Suffill, Kutasi, Pickering & Branigan, 2021), or that alignment at multiple levels is needed to boost communicative success. It may also be the case that laboratory tasks elicit relatively unchallenging conversational exchanges and thus fail to uncover possible benefits of alignment. Interestingly, Reitter and Moore (2014) found evidence supporting the alignment hypothesis in rich and unsupervised task-driven dialogues between conversational partners completing the Map Task, that is, a task where one participant gives instructions for drawing a route on a map to another participant and thus where alignment of situation models is critical for task success. Participants who showed more long-term (but not short-term) structural alignment in this task had more similar paths. Drawing causal inferences about the role of abstract syntax from these data is complicated, but the relationship between long-term linguistic adaptation and task performance suggests that alignment needs to be tracked over longer time intervals than is typically done in the lab. Designing suitable tasks to detect such effects is a methodological challenge that we return to in Section 4.1.

2.3 Conclusions

In sum, the evidence on lexical or abstract syntactic control of grammatical encoding from structural priming paradigms is mixed. On the one hand, there is support for the psychological reality of abstract syntax in studies showing syntactic influences on structure choice; on the other hand, there is also evidence of non-syntactic influences on structure choice in similar sentences. The magnitude of lexically supported structural repetition effects is often larger than that of lexically unsupported repetition but has a shorter lifespan. On balance, while the generation of syntactic structures may not be fully lexically independent, there are clear limits to lexical effects. These limits are crucial for determining key architectural properties of production models, both for monolingual and bilingual speakers, such as the separation of the content and sequencing systems in the Dual Path model (Chang et al., 2006), and key processing parameters, such as determining the weights assigned to thematic roles in these models. The next section considers the question of lexical and syntactic influences on grammatical encoding by tracking the time-course of sentence planning.

3 The Time-Course of Grammatical Encoding: Planning Scope

The fluent production of spoken sentences requires speakers to plan ahead, both in terms of grammatical structures and lexical content. As reviewed above, theories differ in how they model the interdependence between these processes. What is undisputed is that utterances are not usually fully planned prior to articulation. According to the incrementality proposal (e.g., Kempen & Hoenkamp, 1987; Levelt, 1989, 1992; Levelt et al., 1999), utterances are generated in a piecemeal fashion, allowing speakers to output early parts of an utterance while planning upcoming parts. Incrementality means that each sequential processing stage can be initiated based on only a piece of information from the preceding stage, thereby allowing for parallel processing of different parts of an utterance at different levels of representation. For example, incremental processing would allow a speaker to articulate the initial portion of their utterance while grammatically and conceptually encoding upcoming parts.

A fully specified incremental model of speech production should state what determines the scope of advanced planning, that is, how much of an utterance is generated at a particular level of representation before processing at the next level can begin. However, the degree to which grammatical planning is completed prior to utterance onset remains a matter for debate. Allowing small increments to planning prior to speech onset, for example lexical increments, would of course facilitate the speed of output and reduce memory costs. However, incremental systems must also have processes that determine the order in which different utterance parts should be encoded to reduce linearisation errors. Such ordering processes should be influenced by the grammatical systems of the target language, as languages differ in terms of how, and how flexibly, syntactic units can be ordered (e.g., Allum & Wheeldon, 2007, 2009; Hwang & Kaiser, 2014a; Momma et al., 2016; Norcliffe et al., 2015; Myachykov, Scheepers, Garrod, Thompson & Fedorova, 2013; Sauppe, Norcliffe & Konopka, van Valin & Levinson, 2013). For example, Myachykov and colleagues (2013) observed a broader planning scope in the more syntactically flexible language Russian than in English.

Planning scope will also be affected by different backward dependencies in languages, such as obligatory morphological markers that link lexical representations within phrases. For example, determiners and adjectives in NPs are marked for noun gender in Norwegian (e.g., 'et rødt hus' indefinite neuter, 'en rød bil' indefinite masculine); therefore, the correct form of the determiner and adjective is dependent on the gender of the upcoming noun. Moreover, as discussed in Section 1.1.4, not all grammatical dependencies occur locally within a phrase but can cross clause boundaries (e.g., Momma, 2021. 2022; Sarvasy, Morgan, Yu, Ferreira & Momma, 2022). There are also questions about the representation and planning of backward dependencies due to collocational factors (e.g., strong coffee/powerful computer) and idiomatic phrases (e.g., 'kick the bucket'), which must be represented and processed as complete units at some level (e.g., Smith, 2000). However, idioms also differ in the degree to which they can be adapted syntactically (e.g., Fellbaum, 2019) and, as was discussed above (Section 2.1), there is strong evidence from structural priming studies that grammatical encoding processes function in a similar way during the production of idiomatic and non-idiomatic utterances (Konopka & Bock, 2009).

Current models of grammatical encoding make very different predictions about planning units. Some lexically driven models (e.g., Bock & Levelt, 1994; Garrett, 1980a, b; Levelt, 1989) require verb subcategorisation information to assign content words to grammatical functions and to initiate structure generation. These models therefore propose a clausal scope for grammatical encoding. Other approaches also give verbs a central role in planning but with some restrictions (e.g., Momma et al., 2016; Momma, Slevc, & Phillips, 2018, discussed in Section 3.1) and allow abstract syntactic structures to interact with lexical representations to guide planning (e.g., Momma, 2021). In contrast, the Dual Path model of Chang and colleagues (described in Section 1.1.4) proposes that the integration of lexical content into syntactic structures proceeds on a word-by-word basis guided by the mapping of thematic to syntactic structures. Of course, the planning scope for lexical and syntactic processes need not coincide and may vary according to a number of factors, both linguistic and non-linguistic, requiring more flexible and adaptive models of grammatical encoding (e.g., Dell & Jacobs, 2016). In this section, we review the evidence for the scope of advanced planning in grammatical encoding and of the linguistic and cognitive factors that can determine it.

3.1 Evidence for Grammatical Planning Scope: Effects of Linguistic Structure

The first evidence for planning units came from studies of pausing and speech errors (e.g., Butterworth, 1980; Bock & Cutting, 1992; Garrett, 1980a; Goldman Eisler, 1968). However, in order to investigate the time-course of grammatical planning, a variety of online methodologies have been employed. Many studies have focused on measures of lexical processing during production of utterances consisting of NPs (e.g., 'The hat and the tree ...'). Early eye-tracking studies of object naming showed evidence for a radically incremental lexical planning scope. The objects to be described were fixated one-by-one in the order of mention, and fixation durations were affected by the conceptual, lexical and phonological properties of the picture name and not by properties of the picture named next (Griffin, 2001, Levelt & Meyer, 2000; Meyer, Sleiderink & Levelt 1998; Meyer, Wheeldon, van de Meulen & Konopka, 2012). The timing of the first fixation to the next picture was slightly in advance of the articulation of the preceding picture name. The data were consistent with the first picture being processed to the level of phonological encoding prior to gaze shifting to the next picture. However, Meyer and colleagues (2012) also demonstrated that, with increased practice, the time between the shift of gaze from an object and the articulation of its name becomes shorter, and there is also evidence of the peripheral processing of upcoming pictures to be named (e.g., Morgan & Meyer, 2005; Schotter, Ferreira & Rayner, 2013), suggesting a greater degree of advanced planning. Moreover, in these studies, the same structure was used on all trials (e.g., *the hat and the tree*), minimising the effect of conceptual and grammatical structure on planning. With the production of more variable syntactic structures, object-by-object fixations are usually preceded by an initial scan of the visual scene, suggesting more extensive processing of the visual display (e.g., Griffin & Bock, 2000). Exactly what information is retrieved, and which representations are constructed based on this initial scan, remains a matter of debate, to which we return later in this section.

A number of experimental sentence production studies have provided evidence suggestive of grammatical constraints on planning scope. Levelt and Maassen (1981) asked participants to describe displays of moving shapes and found that latencies to initiate description with coordinate NPs such as '*The circle and the square move up*', were longer than for descriptions involving

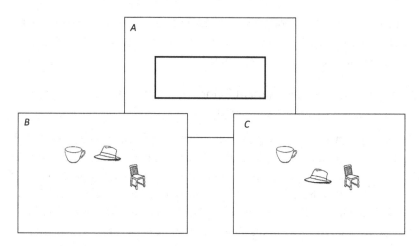

The cup and the hat move above the chair   *The cup moves above the hat and the chair*

Figure 4 Example stimuli from Smith and Wheeldon (1999, Experiment 1). Trials began with a warning frame (A) for 500 ms followed by a blank screen for 500 ms. A horizontal array of pictures then appeared, some of which immediately began to move (2.5 cm in 600 ms). Participants were instructed to describe the array from left to right. To-be-produced sentences thus comprised either a coordinate NP followed by a simple NP (B) or the reverse (C). Pictures from Cycowicz et al (1997)

coordinate sentences such as '*The circle moves up and the square moves up*'. The coordinate sentence structures are longer and more complex than the coordinate NPs but were initiated more quickly – a finding consistent with incremental planning of the first clause ('the circle moves up') or phrase ('the circle') during the production of the coordinate sentences. Smith and Wheeldon (1999) used an extended version of this methodology in order to determine whether the clause or the phrase defined the planning scope during fluent sentence production. Clearly not all speech is fluent, but the aim of these studies was to investigate the optimal time-course for incremental planning, that is, how the system operates when everything is going well. Their studies included a large number of simple line drawings of objects (ninety-two in total) and used filler trials to vary the sentence structures produced over the course of the experiment. Experimental trials involved a horizonal row of three pictured objects that moved up or down. The task was to describe the display from left to right as quickly and fluently as possible. As shown in Figure 4, correct descriptions were single clauses of equal complexity, comprising both coordinate and simple NPs but differing in which phrase type was produced first.

Fluent and correct utterances beginning with coordinate NPs were initiated significantly more slowly than utterances beginning with simple NPs (a difference of 77 ms). This finding is inconsistent with both lexical and clausal planning scopes, instead suggesting that speakers planned the first phrase prior to speech onset. This finding was replicated by Martin, Miller and Vu (2004; see also Martin & Freedman, 2001), who also tested two aphasic patients (ML, EA) to show that the processing of complex NPs caused a marked processing disadvantage for the patient with a short-term memory disadvantage in semantic retention (ML) but not for the patient with a deficit in phonological retention (EA). Martin and colleagues (2004) argued that the effect was therefore occurring during planning of lexical semantics (see also Martin, 2021; Martin & Schnur, 2019). More recently, the Smith and Wheeldon (1999) methodology has been used to demonstrate a phrasal planning scope in both the dominant and non-dominant languages of bilingual speakers (Li, Ferreira & Gollan, 2022). Moreover, when speakers were required to switch languages to name the second picture in the displays, switch costs (in terms of speech-duration measures) were observed later in the simple–complex than the complex–simple sentences. The first noun and determiner showed longer production latencies in the initial complex NPs in the language-switch trials, whereas similar switch costs occurred only on the second noun or just prior to it in the simple NP sentences. These findings are consistent with phrasal planning occurring prior to language-switch planning in bilingual sentence production.

Importantly, the effect of phrase size observed using the Smith and Wheeldon (1999) methodology cannot be attributed to effects of visual complexity, that is, the grouping of pictures visually rather than syntactically, as it is not observed when speakers are asked to name the pictures left to right rather than to produce a sentence (Martin, Crowther, Knight, Tamborello & Yang, 2010; see also Wheeldon & Meyer, 2005). Of course, the phrase complexity effect might be driven by the predictability of the verb. If, for example, speakers prefer to retrieve at least two content words prior to speech onset, then a simple NP will be easier to plan because the second content word is always the same verb ('moves'). This possibility was ruled out by Martin and colleagues (2010), who replicated the effect with varying verbs. The effect is also observed in a verb-final language such as Japanese. Allum and Wheeldon (2007) used coloured picture displays to elicit sentences such as 11a and 11b below. This experiment also ruled out an explanation of the phrase complexity effect in terms of phonological planning. The generation of the phonological structure of utter-ances is also an incremental process, and there is evidence for the phonological word as a planning unit (Wheeldon & Lahiri, 1997, 2002; Wynne, Wheeldon & Lahiri, 2018). A phonological word comprises a lexical word plus any follow-ing unstressed syllables. The coordinate phrases in the English sentences begin with a larger phonological word (e.g., 'the cup and the') than the simple sentences (e.g., 'the cup'). However, this is not true of the Japanese sentences in 11, which are perfectly matched for initial phonological word structure.

11. a. [INU to BOUSHI wa] FOOKU no ue ni arimasu
        [Dog and hat TOP] fork above are
        The dog and the hat are above the fork
     b. [INU wa] BOUSHI to FOOKU no ue ni arimasu
        [Dog TOP] hat and fork above is
        The dog is above the hat and the fork

The relative contributions of conceptual and syntactic structure to phrasal scope effects are more difficult to untangle. The relationship between the thematic structure to be expressed and the unfolding syntactic structure that is constructed to express it is not simple. Nevertheless, these representations will, of course, share many structural features. In the simple-sentence structures tested in the studies described above, the sentence-initial phrases represent key units at both conceptual (agent or theme) and grammatical (subject phrase, and head of the subject phrase) levels. Allum and Wheeldon (2007) tested the production of utterances with complex subject phrases which included a modifying prepositional phrase such as 'The cup above the hat is blue'. These sentences were initiated approximately 100 ms faster than coordinate NP sentences (e.g., 'the cup and the hat are blue') in which both simple NPs act as hierarchically equal heads. This pattern is inconsistent with the scope of planning being the entire subject phrase and suggests instead that speakers planned only the head of the subject phrase prior to speech onset. The generation of similar sentences in Japanese was tested in order to determine whether the initial unit was determined at a grammatical (head of initial phrase) or a conceptual level (theme) of representation (Experiment 2). Unlike English, Japanese is a head-final language, in which a modifying prepositional phrase occurs before the head of a subject phrase (see Figure 5). In a head-final language, therefore, the first grammatical phrase is not necessarily the theme of the sentence. This allows us to determine whether conceptual salience or grammatical convention governs processing scope. The stimuli for this experiment varied the size of the sentence-initial prepositional phrase while keeping the size of the subject phrase as a whole constant. Latencies increased by approximately 50 ms with each lexical addition to the prepositional phrase, a finding consistent with Japanese speakers planning the sentence-initial phrase prior to speech onset rather than the whole subject phrase. Critically, this phrase does not encode a major or the most salient thematic unit. The sentence-initial phrase is determined by Japanese syntax and is therefore consistent with a grammatical encoding locus for the phrasal scope effect.

Figure 5 Example stimuli from Allum and Wheeldon (2007, Experiment 3). The picture stimuli elicited Japanese sentences with an initial modifying prepositional phrase comprising one, two or three nouns. As the side of the prepositional phrase increased the size of the head of the subject phrase decreased, maintaining a fixed size for the subject phrase across the three conditions. Naming latencies and percentage error rates for the three conditions are shown, as well as the latency increase associated with the increasing initial phrase size. pictures from Cycowicz et al (1997)

Grammatical encoding has two main component processes: lemma retrieval and structure building, but how do these processes contribute to the scope effect? Does phrase structure determine the scope of lexical access prior to articulation? This is an important question as it has consequences for modelling the mapping between conceptual and grammatical units. As reviewed in Section 1.1.4, theories of grammatical encoding differ in the degree to which they are led by lexical or structural representations. In lexically driven models (Bock and Levelt, 1994; Levelt, 1989, 1992; Pickering and Branigan, 1998), the order of lexical activation is determined by the conceptual weighting of lexical concepts. A highly activated lexical concept will activate its associated lemma and this in turn will influence function assignment and the syntactic structure to be generated. For example, if the patient concept 'Bill' in our example above was the most highly activated, the lemma for 'Bill' might be assigned the grammatical subject function, resulting in a passive sentence ('Bill was seen by Anne'). Indeed, the salience of lexical concepts can affect structural choice (e.g., Bock, 1986; Gleitman, January, Nappa & Trueswell, 2007), although most significantly when event encoding is difficult (Kuchinsky & Bock, 2010). Moreover, the effect of salience has also been shown to be subject to language-specific grammatical constraints (e.g., Hwang & Kaiser, 2015; Myachykov, Garrod & Scheepers, 2010; Myachykov, Garrod & Scheepers, 2018; Myachykov, Thompson, Scheepers & Garrod, 2011; Myachykov & Tomlin, 2008; but see Schlenter, Esaulova, Dolscheid & Penke, 2022, for a null effect of case marking). Many studies have now shown that the order of lexical activation is driven by the requirements of a given structure (e.g., active or passive sentences; Griffin & Bock, 2000) or of the structural requirements of a given particular language (e.g., Hwang & Kaiser, 2014b; Momma et al, 2016; Norcliffe et al., 2015; Sauppe et al., 2013).

If the scope of grammatical encoding is the sentence-initial phrase, the question then arises of how a non-linear thematic structure controls the order of lemma activation for initial phrases with no conceptual weighting, such as the modifying phrase 'above the crab' in Japanese (Figure 5). If the sentence-initial phrase also determines the minimal scope of lexical retrieval, then, arguably, it must be possible for syntactic and thematic processes to interact to determine the order of lexical access. In the Dual Path model (Chang, 2002; Chang et al., 2006), syntactic structure is generated based on the thematic structure and learned syntactic rules independently of the retrieval of lexical content. The TAG model (Momma, 2021) also has mechanisms by which some thematic and syntactic structures can interact directly and independently of lexical content. Allum and Wheeldon (2009; see also Wheeldon, 2012) investigated this issue using a picture-preview paradigm in which one of the pictures to be named on a picture-description trial was previewed for one second prior to the onset of the picture to be described. Picture preview occurred on a third of all trials and participants knew only that the previewed picture would always occur in the upcoming display but not where it would occur in the display or in the sentence description. Both native English and Japanese speakers produced picture descriptions such as 12a–d below and the previewed pictures were either the first or the second objects to be mentioned.

12. a. [The fork] above the dog is blue
     b. [Inu no ue no] fooku wa ao desu
     c. [Inu to fooku wa] ao desu
     d. [The dog and the fork] are blue

The prediction was that picture preview should facilitate sentence production only if the picture name was required for utterance planning prior to speech onset. If the scope of lexical access is determined by phrase structure, then during the production of the prepositional subjected phrases in 12a and 12b, a preview benefit should be observed only for the first noun to be produced in speakers of both English and Japanese – even though the initial noun plays different grammatical roles in each language. This was the effect observed. In contrast, both the first and second nouns in the coordinate NP sentences such as 12c and 12d showed significant preview benefits, although they were significantly larger for the first than for the second nouns. The pattern of picture-preview benefits therefore matches the phrasal scope finding reviewed above and suggests that a phrasal scope determines the scope of lexical access prior to speech onset.

The structural nature of the picture-preview effects was confirmed in an experiment which tested two different forms of coordination in Japanese with different conceptual and syntactic characteristics (Allum & Wheeldon, 2009). The to-wa coordination used in the previous experiments binds the coordinates as a set and is usually contrastive. So, for example, the sentences in 12d above suggests that the dog and the fork are blue in contrast to the colour of other objects. An alternative form of coordination is mo-mo (e.g., '[Inu mo fooku mo] ao desu'), which binds items more loosely conceptually and syntactically. Mo-mo functions as a listing form of coordination and is not contrastive, that is, the dog and the fork are blue as well as other objects. The different forms of coordination also have consequences for the scope of application of adjectives. In a sentence such as 'the blue cup and plate are broken', with to-wa coordination both objects are blue, but with mo-mo coordination only the cup is blue. These structural differences would predict differences in planning scope. Using the same visual displays as for the to-wa experiments described above, the mo-mo coordination showed no preview benefit for the second picture to be named.

Defining the syntactic unit determining the phrasal scope effect is, however, not straightforward. The coordinate NPs need not correspond to a salient thematic unit or to a major grammatical phrase such as the subject phrase or even its head. They also do not correspond to a minimal grammatical phrase as coordinate NPs, which are constructed from two simple phrases, are planned as a unit. Allum and Wheeldon (2007; see also Zhao, Alario & Yang, 2014) suggested that some reference to thematic structure is required in order to define the phrasal unit, which also needs to function as a minimal thematic unit in the message.

The picture-preview experiments provide evidence that the phrasal scope determines the lower limit of lexical planning prior to articulation. As argued above, this finding suggests that higher-level conceptual-syntactic representations are constructed prior to (and thus guide) lexical access. This is consistent with the Dual Path model, which allows direct mapping from thematic to grammatical structure in order to ensure the correct order of word retrieval model (Chang, et al., 2006; also Konopka & Bock, 2009). But what is the nature of the guiding syntactic representation? Although processing of the initial phrase is prioritised prior to speech onset, there is also clear evidence of more global processing beyond the initial phrase. Griffin and Bock (2000; see also Konopka, 2012, 2019; Van de Velde, Meyer & Konopka, 2014) argued that, when describing event pictures spontaneously, initial gazes are not predictive of what speakers will say (e.g., they are not predictive of structure choice) but rather reflect a gist apprehension phase that involves encoding a conceptual structure of the pictured event prior to the onset of linguistic encoding. Konopka (2019) investigated the time-course of the planning of relational information in simple sentences (e.g., 'The tiger is scratching the photographer'), that is, planning of the main action of the event at the message level (i.e., scratching) as well as the verb (i.e., 'scratching') to express this action at the sentence level. In two eye-tracking experiments, speakers described pictured events in response to questions that were either neutral (e.g., 13a) or focused the speaker on the agent (13b) or the patient (13c) in the event. Agents and patient characters were either more or less informative about the action being performed.

13. a. Neutral: What is happening?
     b. Agent-focused: What is the tiger doing?
     c. Patient-focused: What is happening to the photographer?

Neutral questions elicited 77 per cemt active sentences, whereas the focused questions (13b and 13c) elicited almost exclusively active and passive sentences, respectively. Eye movements were analysed in two time windows based on previous studies, which have shown that fixations in the first 400 ms of a trial are related to message planning and that fixations thereafter are related to linguistic planning (Gleitman et al., 2007; Griffin & Bock, 2000; Konopka & Meyer, 2014; Konopka et al., 2018). In all conditions, eye movements during the 0–400 ms window moved between agents and patients, but with a preference for the character that was more informative for the purpose of encoding the event action, consistent with early relational processing. Effects of the question manipulation were observed in the second window. Following the neutral questions, speakers looked at the two characters in their order of mention, but when answering agent-focused questions, speakers looked at both characters until speech onset (1200 ms) and thereafter they mostly fixated on the patient. This pattern is consistent with conceptual encoding of relational information (necessary for verb retrieval) prior to speech onset, an interpretation supported by a preference to focus on action-informative characters in this time window. In contrast, no such encoding window was observed for passive sentences after patient-focused questions. Instead, speakers fixated on patients followed by agents after 400 ms. Nevertheless, the gaze patterns clearly demonstrate the early extraction of relational information required for hierarchical processing both during message-level planning and the mapping of the message to the required sentence output.

Models of grammatical encoding therefore need to account for the planning of both global and local representations of utterances. As reviewed in Section 1.1.4, the classic lexically driven model of grammatical encoding requires verbs to be retrieved prior to phrase structure building as verbs are required for function assignment (e.g., Bock & Levelt, 1994; Levelt, 1989; Levelt et al., 1999; Pickering & Branigan, 1998). This claim was tested by Schriefers, Teruel and Meinshausen (1998), who used an extended version of the picture–word interference task (Meyer, 1996; Schriefers, Meyer & Levelt, 1990) in which native German speakers produced descriptions of pictured actions like 'The man empties the bucket'. The position of the verb in the picture description was manipulated using lead-in phrases such as those in 14 below.

14. a. SVO   *Der Mann **leert** den Eimer*   *The man **empties** the bucket*

  b. (Auf dem nächsten Bild sieht man wie)   (On the next picture one sees how)

  SOV   *- der Mann den Eimer **leert***   *- the man the bucket **empties**)*

  c. (Und auf dem nechsten Bild)   (And on the next picture)

  VSO   *- **leert** der Mann den Eimer*   *- **empties** the man the bucket)*

Picture onset was accompanied by a semantically related distractor verb (e.g., 'empty') which causes interference and slows naming (Schriefers et al., 1990). Compared to an unrelated distractor verb (e.g., 'writes'), the semantically related distractor caused interference only in the production of VSO sentences (e.g., 15c), suggesting that only verbs in sentence-initial position are retrieved prior to speech onset. However, more recent research suggests that verb retrieval may occur prior to speech onset when their relationship to object arguments, rather than subject arguments, is critical. For example, Momma and colleagues (2016) used the same methodology to test Japanese speakers' production of object-initial and subject-initial sentences and observed semantic interference effects only for object-initial sentences. Other studies have shown evidence that verbs are planned before subject nouns produced in English passive sentences but not active sentences (Momma, Slevc & Phillips, 2015). Momma and colleagues (2018) showed a similar effect in the processing of two different classes of transitive verbs: unaccusative verbs which can only take patients or themes as their argument (e.g., 15a), and unergative verbs, which can only take agents as their argument (15b). Participants learned to produced sentence like those in 15a and 15b as picture descriptions.

15. a. The doctor is *floating* (unaccusative)

  b. The doctor is *sleeping* (unergative)

Written distractor verbs were shown prior to picture onset and were either semantically related or unrelated to the target verb to be produced. A semantic interference effect on sentence onset latencies was observed for the unaccusative verbs but not for the unergative verbs. Spoken duration measures showed the reverse pattern of priming effects, with longer durations for the subject noun +auxilliary in the unergative sentences but not in the unaccusative sentences. This pattern of results is consistent with the unaccusative verbs being planned prior to sentence onset but the unergative verbs being planned during the articulation of the subject noun. Based on these data and on proposals from theoretical linguistics (see Momma & Ferreira, 2021, for a discussion), Momma and colleagues make a distinction between a verb's external (subject) arguments and internal (object) arguments. They propose that verbs only need to be retrieved prior to planning their internal arguments.

There is also evidence that hierarchical planning can cross clause boundaries. Smith and Wheeldon (1999) compared the production of one-clause and two-clause sentences such as in 16 below.

16. a. The cup moves up (one clause)
    b. The cup and the hat move up (one clause)
    c. The cup moves up and the hat and the chair move down (two clauses)
    d. The cup and the hat move up and the chair moves down (two clauses)

The latency benefit for sentences with initial simple phrases was replicated confirming that processing of the initial phrase is prioritised prior to speech onset. However, the two-clause sentences (16c and 16d) took significantly longer to initiate (by 142 ms) than the single-clause sentences (16a and 16b), and the effect of initial phrase size was smaller in the two-clause sentences (78 ms) than the single-clause sentences (195 ms). This pattern of results is consistent with a degree of structural processing of elements in the second clause occurring prior to speech onset, which is also affected by their complexity.

Momma (2021) investigated the planning of long-distance dependencies such as the cross-clause filler-gap dependency in 'Who does the artist think is chasing the ballerina?'. The methodology combined picture descriptions to elicit the target sentences in 17 with a priming manipulation for the use of 'that'. The prime sentences either did or did not contain 'that' (e.g., *The flight attendant thinks (that) the captain will announce something*). They were presented as part of a sentence memorisation phase in which participants saw two sentences sequentially and were subsequently cued to produce one of them. Participants then produced target sentences as descriptions of pictured scenes. The aim was to test for effects of 'that' priming on the production of sentences where 'that' cannot legally occur in a long-distance dependency, such as in 17a versus 17b. The effect of the prime was to slow onset latencies for sentences such as 17a but not 17b, suggesting that the grammatical structure of the dependency is planned prior to speech onset.

17. a. Who does the artist think (*that) is chasing the ballerina?
    b. Who does the artist think (that) the chef is chasing?

The planning of long-distance dependencies and of unaccusative verbs prior to speech onset is in conflict with the evidence for an incremental phrasal planning scope reviewed previously in this section. However, according to the tree adjoining grammar (TAG) model of grammatical encoding, long-distance dependencies can be planned without planning the intervening material, which can be tree-adjoined later. This model therefore provides an explicit mechanism for global structural planning within an incremental grammatical encoding system. Evidence for such a model was provided by Momma and Ferreira (2021), who investigated the time-course of the planning of sentences with unaccusative verbs such as 'The octopus below the spoon is boiling'. They employed the extended picture-word interference paradigm to test for interference from semantic distractors related to the verb (e.g., melt) or to the noun in the modifying prepositional phrase (e.g., knife). Onset latencies to the subject noun (e.g., octopus) were significantly slowed by verb distractors but not by noun distractors, suggesting that the verb, but not the modifying prepositional phrase, was planned prior to subject onset. Unergative verb sentences showed a less consistent pattern of results, with evidence of verb retrieval prior to subject onset in some experiments (in contrast to Momma et al., 2018) and variation across participants suggestive of individual differences in planning scope, a topic discussed in the following section.

In summary, the evidence reviewed in this section shows clear effects of syntactic structure on both the scope and the order of lexical retrieval operations. These effects have been observed for long-distance structural dependencies as well as for local phrase structures. They are consistent with structurally driven rather than lexically driven grammatical encoding processes, and with the generation of global hierarchical syntactic structures prior to the sequential construction of constituent phrases. In the next section, we turn to the evidence that non-linguistic factors might also affect the scope of grammatical encoding.

3.2 Evidence for Flexibility in Planning Scope: Effects of Non-linguistic Factors

Despite its apparent ease, speaking is a cognitively costly activity which can negatively affect, and be affected by, concurrent tasks (e.g., Jongman, Roelofs & Meyer, 2015; Roelofs & Piai, 2011). This raises the possibility that advanced planning could also be constrained by non-linguistic factors due to the nature of the context in which sentences must be produced or be governed by cognitive limitations due to individual differences in attention or working memory. It is also possible that planning scope is to some extent under a speaker's control.

3.2.1 Cognitive Load in Linguistic Processing

Cognitive load can vary within the language planning system due to differences in the ease with which utterance increments can be planned or retrieved at different levels of representation. A number of studies suggest that varying cognitive load can affect the scope of grammatical planning processes. Message-level representations that are easier to construct result in increased planning scopes (e.g., Konopka & Meyer, 2014; Kuchinsky & Bock 2010; van de Velde et al., 2014). Konopka and Meyer (2014) used a spontaneous production task in which speakers described pictures of transitive events eliciting active and passive sentences. Analyses of eye movements during production of active sentences (e.g., 'The dog is chasing the postman') showed that speakers allocated more attention to both characters shortly after picture onset when the gist of the event was easy to encode and to express linguistically (suggesting planning of a larger message, consistent with Hierarchical Incrementality) but quickly directed their attention to the character they would mention first when the gist of the event was more difficult to encode and to express (suggesting planning of a small, one-character increment at the outset of the planning process, consistent with Linear Incrementality). Further, facilitating generation of an active sentence via structural priming also resulted in a shift towards planning of a larger message shortly after picture onset. Such differences across items and shifts in planning strategies due to structural priming suggest that speakers can change planning strategies flexibly and dynamically. Specifically, speakers appear to prioritise processes that can be completed quickly at the outset of planning, so planning may proceed in larger increments or in small increments for different sentences.

Effects of cognitive load on lexical retrieval have also been observed. Word retrieval is a notoriously costly process, prone to retrieval failures (e.g., tip-of-the-tongue states; Brown & McNeil, 1966; Meyer & Bock, 1992) which increase with the learning of addition languages (e.g., Gollan & Acenas, 2004) and in older age (Segaert et al., 2018). As mentioned above, in picture-naming tasks, there is evidence of parallel activation of upcoming picture names (e.g., Schotter, et al., 2013), but also evidence that the pre-activation of upcoming pictures is influenced by the ease of name retrieval (e.g., Konopka, 2012; Malpass & Meyer, 2010; Morgan & Meyer, 2005; Wheeldon et al., 2011). It has further been shown that syntactic processing load can affect lexical planning scope. Lexical processing scope is smaller when the sentence structures to be produced vary from trial to trial (e.g., Wagner et al., 2010). Conversely, lexical planning scope increases when the syntactic processing load is reduced using structural priming (Konopka, 2012, Konopka & Kuchinsky, 2015, Konopka & Meyer, 2014; see Wheeldon & Konopka, 2018, for a review). For example, Konopka (2012) used a structural priming methodology to facilitate the production of sentences beginning with complex NPs that included semantically related or unrelated nouns (e.g., '*The axe and the cup* are above the book' vs. '*The axe and the saw* are above the book'). Lexical planning scope was measured by comparing sentence onsets for the two types of NPs in structurally primed and unprimed conditions, that is, after producing prime sentences beginning with complex NPs or simple NPs (see Smith & Wheeldon, 2001; Wheeldon & Smith, 2003). The results showed earlier retrieval of the second noun when the complex NP structure was primed, as evidenced by the presence of semantic interference delaying sentence onsets, but not when the structure was unprimed. However, increases in lexical planning scope were not observed beyond the initial phrase.

A related question is the extent to which lexical availability can affect syntactic planning scope. Retrieving and buffering words in memory is cognitively demanding, so can speakers extend their syntactic processing scope to encompass available lexical material? Wheeldon, Ohlson, Ashby and Gator (2013) tested this by manipulating both lexical availability and initial phrase structure at the same time. Speakers saw a previewed picture followed by an array of four moving pictures, which again elicited sentences beginning with a coordinate or a simple NP. In the critical sentences, the previewed picture was always the second picture to be named. The position of the previewed picture was either unpredictable (i.e., filler trials were used to vary the position) or predictable (always occurring in second position in experimental *and* filler sentences). Unpredictable preview replicated the benefit for pictures falling within the initial phrase but not beyond it, as observed by Allum and Wheeldon (2009). When preview was predictable, a significant benefit was observed for pictures beyond the first phrase, as well as a significant effect of initial phrase length. This pattern of results is consistent with speakers extending their planning to include some processing of the second picture in a display when it is previewed but is not consistent with the picture's name being retrieved and incorporated into the grammatical structure prior to speech onset. Interestingly, the effect of picture preview beyond the first phrase was shown to be inhibitory rather than facilitatory in older adults (Hardy et al., 2020), suggesting age-related differences in the ability to hold on to upcoming lexical information while planning sentence-initial phrases. Finally, Wheeldon and colleagues (2013) observed no preview benefit for the predictable preview of pictures occurring in the final position of three of a three-noun coordinate phrase, although the effect of initial phrase length (between a two-noun and three-noun coordinate) was significant. Along with similar findings reviewed above (e.g., Konopka, 2012), this demonstrates that initial phrase structure does not necessarily determine the upper limit of lexical access, confirming that phrasal and lexical processing scope do not necessarily coincide (see Roeser, Torrance & Baguley, 2019, for similar findings in the planning of written phrases).

Language experience and proficiency also affect the cognitive demands of speaking, and studies of bilingual language planning have shown that planning scope can differ in a bilingual's dominant and non-dominant language (e.g., Gilbert, Cousineau-Perusse, & Titone, 2020; Konopka et al., 2018). For example, Konopka and colleagues (2018) compared planning of active SVO sentences (e.g., 'The dog is chasing the postman') by Dutch speakers with high proficiency in English. Analyses of eye movements before speech onset showed that the speakers began fixating and thus linguistically encoding the sentence-initial character (the agent: 'The dog . . .') earlier when generating a description in Dutch than in English. Early encoding of the sentence-initial noun implies that speakers allocated fewer resources to the advance planning of the information to be produced next ('. . . is chasing the postman'), that is, that they engaged in more linearly incremental planning rather than in hierarchical planning. Thus, speakers were more likely to adopt an opportunistic (or risky, on-the-fly) planning strategy when using their native language, possibly because they would be able to plan subsequent conceptual and linguistic increments (verbs and the patient names) quickly or would be able to correct any errors if they ran into problems from their chosen starting point ('The dog . . .'). By comparison, production is more effortful in a second language, so a highly incremental, risky planning strategy is not optimal: when preparing English sentences, speakers allocated more resources to encoding information about the whole event before beginning linguistic encoding of the sentence-initial character, consistent with a hierarchically incremental planning strategy. Konopka and colleagues (2018) verified that this effect was indeed due to speakers' preference to encode relational (verb-related) information early in the planning process rather than due only to a delay in retrieving the sentence-initial referent name.

3.2.2 Individual Differences in Cognitive Abilities

The evidence reviewed in the previous section demonstrates that cognitive load can influence grammatical planning scope within the language system.

These findings raise the question of whether individual differences in cognitive abilities can have similar effects. There is some evidence for effects on language planning of individual differences in cognitive abilities related to attention and memory. Arguably, cognitive limitations might necessitate the adoption of smaller, less demanding planning increments (e.g., Christiansen & Chater, 2016). For example, there is evidence of a relationship between working memory (WM) capacity and planning scope (e.g., Martin et al., 2004; Martin & Slevc, 2014). A number of studies have demonstrated that higher performance in WM tasks is related to planning of larger increments (e.g., Petrone, Fuchs & Krivovokapić, 2011; Swets, Desmet, Hambrick, & Ferreira, 2007; Swets, Fuchs, Krivovokapić & Petrone, 2021; Swets et al., 2014). For example, Petrone and colleagues (2011) demonstrated a relationship between WM capacity and phrase-initial fundamental frequency (F0, the acoustic measure related to pitch). Phrase-initial F0 was higher for speakers with high WM than for those with low WM. There is a decline in F0 across an utterance, and longer phrases are initiated with a higher F0 than shorter phrases, suggesting that phrase-initial F0 is a measure of planning scope (see also Fuchs, Petrone, Krivokapić & Hoole, 2013). In a different approach, Swets and colleagues (2014) related individual differences in WM to speakers' performance in an interactive speech production task in which participants directed a listener to move pictured objects in grids on a screen. Speakers with better WM performance showed evidence of a broader planning scope in this task. They were more likely to look at the third object in a scene (e.g., a wheel) prior to initiating a sentence such as 'The cat moves below the train and the wheel moves above the train'. They were also more likely to produce disambiguating modifications to the first NP such as 'The four-legged cat moves below the train ... .'. Onset latencies to contrasting sentence structures did not vary for low- and high-WM speakers; however, these data suggest that high-WM speakers were able to plan further ahead than low-WM speakers within the same time frame. In a follow-up study, Swets and colleagues (2021) investigated whether differences in language requirements interact with individual differences in cognitive factors, such as WM and processing speed. Using a similar methodology to Swets and colleagues (2014), they tested speakers of English, French and German. English and German are Germanic languages that allow modifiers in NPs to occur before or after the noun (e.g., 'the four-legged cat', 'the cat with four legs'). In contrast, modifiers in French are almost always post-nominal (e.g., 'le chat à quatre pattes'). Previous research has shown faster latencies for the planning of post-nominal modification (Brown-Schmidt & Konopka, 2008; Myachykov et al., 2013), suggesting more incremental planning of such phrases. Swets and colleagues (2021) also found evidence for more incremental planning in French speakers than in English and German speakers. French speakers also showed a relationship between speech latency and individual differences in processing speed, which was not observed in the Germanic language speakers. However, the data patterns were not robust, and the relationship between WM and planning scope observed by Swets and colleagues (2014) for English speakers did not replicate. Nevertheless, the study is the first to address the possibility that cognitive capabilities may differ in the extent to which they predict planning scope in speakers of different languages.

Finally, attention is a multifaceted ability (Miyake et al., 2000) and individual differences in some components of attention predict picture-naming performance (Piai & Roelofs, 2013; Shao, Roelofs & Meyer, 2012). In phrase production, the ability to sustain attention has been shown to affect production latencies (e.g., Jongman, Meyer & Roelofs 2015; Jongman, Roelofs & Meyer, 2015). For example, Jongman, Meyer and Roelofs (2015) measured individual differences in sustained attention using a continuous processing task (CPT) involving the monitoring of a series of digits for the target digit 0. Single digits were presented for 100 ms and participants made a button-press response to the target digit. Participants with lower CPT performance also showed an increase in their number of slow responses in the production of conjoined NPs in L1 Dutch (e.g., 'de wortel en de emmer', i.e., the carrot and the bucket), consistent with the effect of lapses of attention. A similar correlation was shown when single-picture naming was followed by a non-linguistic arrow-categorisation task. The findings suggest that speakers need to maintain attention when coordinating the production of NPs, either with another NP or a non-linguistic task. While these results do not speak directly to effects of sustained attention on processing scope, they highlight the need to account for individual differences in cognition in language planning research.

3.2.3 Cognitive Load in Dialogue

Finally, most sentences are spoken in conversational contexts which demand much more than the planning of one's own utterances. An interlocutor must comprehend the speech of other speakers, keep track of what they have said, and constantly update their representation of the unfolding discourse. These processes are demanding of both attention and memory (e.g., Barthel & Sauppe, 2019; Fairs, Bögels & Meyer, 2018; Fargier & Laganaro, 2016). Moreover, timing in conversational turn-taking is very tight, with a new speaker often taking the floor about 200 ms from the offset of the previous speaker's utterance (e.g., Levinson & Torreira, 2015). This raises the possibility that speakers may reduce their processing scope in order to speed up utterance onset under conversational time pressure. However, the literature on turn-taking focuses on the degree to which utterance planning occurs in parallel with listening to the current speaker, rather than on changes in planning scope (e.g., Barthel, Sauppe, Levinson & Meyer, 2016; Lindsay, Gambi & Rabagliati, 2019; Sjerps & Meyer, 2015) and there is evidence that the speed of turn-taking might be overestimated (e.g., Corps, Knudsen & Meyer, 2022). Some studies have shown that pause length in turn-taking is sensitive to measures of the length of the utterance to be produced (e.g., Roberts, Torreira & Levinson, 2015; Torreira, Bögels & Levinson, 2015), but the effect of conversational constraints on the scope of grammatical encoding remains poorly understood. Nevertheless, it remains true that, in order to keep the floor in a conversation, it is important to avoid long planning pauses between one's own utterances, and there is some experimental evidence that planning scope can be reduced under conditions of increased time pressure (e.g., Ferreira & Swets, 2002).

3.3 Conclusions

The studies reviewed above show that a complex pattern of linguistic and non-linguistic factors can influence the time-course of grammatical encoding. In general, the data show more consistent effects of structure planning and more variable effects of lexical planning. Many factors affecting the ease of structural planning influence the scope of lexical retrieval. Conversely, lexical availability does not affect the scope of grammatical encoding even when speakers know the linear order of the available words in the utterance to be produced. Moreover, it is clear that structural and lexical planning scopes do not necessarily coincide. These findings are consistent with a model in which conceptual and syntactic structure can interact to determine the order of lexical activation but where the extent of lexical activation can vary due to factors affecting the ease of planning and to individual differences in cognitive processes.

4 Summing up

4.1 Methodological Review

Research in any area is only as good as the experimental paradigms and data-collection methods allow. A recurring dilemma in language production research is choosing paradigms and stimuli that elicit the desired linguistic output as spontaneously as possible while maintaining a high degree of experimental control. Because language processes unfold very quickly and competing theories make explicit predictions about what type of information is encoded when, good timing resolution is necessary for drawing inferences about the temporal coordination of lexical and structural processes. In addition, many research questions require detailed analysis of participants' speech output (e.g., to relate word onsets to eye movements). In the absence of automatic language analysis tools, this is an extremely time-consuming and labour-intensive process. This issue is also magnified by a second recurring challenge concerning the sheer volume of data needed for appropriately powered comparisons. As in other fields, increasing power usually means recruiting larger samples of participants rather than increasing the size of item pools. Moreover, the most appropriate means for estimating power remains a matter of debate. One notable strength of the field is that it is characterised by a habit of replication which provides important information about effect reliability. However, the field is still prone to reporting biases due to the problems associated with publishing null effects. The growing use of Open Science Framework practices is of critical importance here.

4.1.1 Paradigms

Picture-naming paradigms that elicit simple sentences consisting of NPs (e.g., 'The A and the B') meet the criteria outlined above as these sentences are relatively easy to elicit without training. Studies employing such paradigms have provided much of the initial evidence about vertical information flow in the production system (i.e., top-down information flow as well as feedback from lower levels to higher levels in the lexicon) and horizontal information flow (i.e., estimates of the amount of information that can be planned in parallel at the message level and sentence level). However, the production of more complex sentences is needed to address theoretical issues such as planning of long-distance dependencies. To elicit complex structures, picture-naming studies present participants with hand-drawn pictures or photographs showing transitive or dative events (Griffin & Bock, 2000; Konopka et al., 2018; Segaert, Wheeldon & Hagoort, 2016). Often, picture-naming studies include training blocks where participants are taught to use specific words prior to starting the main production task, or participants are shown printed words to be used in their picture descriptions on a trial-by-trial basis (e.g., Hartsuiker and colleagues; Ziegler & Snedeker, 2018). Studies eliciting sentences that communicate messages that are hard to depict employ sentence memory tasks: sentences are presented to participants either in full or word by word, and the task for participants is to then repeat these sentences back from memory after a short interval (e.g., Ferreira, 2003; Konopka & Bock, 2009; Momma, 2022). Despite evidence that speakers will reproduce these sentences from a gist representation (rather than repeating sentences verbatim from information stored in working memory), the prior processing of the full structure may still have consequences for planning scope that differ from more spontaneous sentence production methodologies.

These paradigms are far from exhaustive in terms of capturing the complexity of language produced outside of the lab. Nevertheless, they have provided data that, so far, can be only partially accounted for by existing computational models. A promising approach for future research is to adapt such paradigms for use in dialogue settings to be able to test effects of interactivity and conversational history.

4.1.2 Dependent Measures

Studies using priming paradigms, such as the structural priming paradigm, have typically relied on two dependent measures: binary outcomes in each trial (such as repetition of the primed structure or production of the unprimed structure), which are aggregated to compute the magnitude of the priming effect across conditions, and onset latencies in the sentences with primed and unprimed structures, which are aggregated to compute facilitation effects across conditions. The former provides a measure of changes in the degree to which the production system is biased to select one structure over another (see Section 2: Bock, 1986; Chang et al., 2006; Pickering & Branigan, 1998), and is typically used to make claims about learning of a structural alteration. The latter provides a continuous measure of how quickly a particular structural procedure can be implemented (Konopka, 2012; Smith & Wheeldon, 1999), regardless of whether speakers select the primed or unprimed structure, and provide key insight into the planning process (Section 3).

Comparisons of sentence latencies across priming conditions are also particularly useful for assessing the effects of structural primes on sentences with preferred structures, that is, sentences that are hard to prime. For example, speakers overwhelmingly prefer to use active syntax than passive syntax. Given that selection of active syntax is often at ceiling, structural primes rarely increase selection of active syntax further (frequent structural alternatives also show less priming; Jaeger & Snider, 2013). However, priming in active sentences is observable with a different measure: sentences that repeat active syntax have shorter onset latencies (Segaert et al., 2014). This suggests that repetition of structure can have facilitatory effects on production in the absence of changes in structure choice. At the same time, sentence onsets are highly sensitive to a large number of variables that influence the speed with which speakers produce linguistic output under any conditions (e.g., lexical constraints such as the ease of retrieving individual content words) as well as changes specific to structural repetition itself, such as structure-driven changes in planning scope (Konopka, 2012; Konopka & Meyer, 2014).

A particularly informative approach in sentence planning is the use of eye tracking to track spontaneous production of sentences that can be elicited with visual stimuli. Sentence onsets vary across studies but speakers rarely begin speaking before 1000 ms. Tracking participants' eye movements provides a rich implicit record of what information participants began encoding at different points in time and how easy this information was to encode *before speech onset*. This is especially relevant for making inferences about incremental planning (see Norcliffe & Konopka, 2015). The richness of the eye-movement record in spontaneous sentence production also presents a challenge: eye movements can capture effects of low-level non-linguistic variables (such as perceptual salience) as well as higher-level linguistic variables (such as message-level encoding difficulty). The time windows in which these variables are likely to influence production in theoretically interesting ways, as well as the way that eye movements reflect an influence of these variables, are still debated (see e.g., Griffin & Davison, 2011; Konopka, 2019).

4.2 Summary and Future Directions

In the opening sections of this Element, we set the processes of grammatic encoding for speech production in context, and we outlined its component processes: lexical retrieval and structure building. The end point of successful grammatical encoding is a representation of appropriate linear order of the words to be phonologically and phonetically encoded for articulation. The theoretical issue that we focused on throughout this Element is the relationship between lexical and structural representations and processes during grammatical encoding. Current models make different claims about lexically driven and structurally driven influences on the linearisation process – that is, if, how and when they interact. We characterised the problem in terms of two theoretical extremes which approximate the claims of lexically driven and structurally driven accounts of grammatical planning: Linear Incrementality and Hierarchical Incrementality. In Linear Incrementality, lexical access is driven by the activation of lexical concepts, and sequencing occurs based on syntactic information represented in lemmas. In Hierarchical Incrementality, syntactic structure is constructed based on thematic relationships in the conceptual structure without reference to lexical content. This structure then drives the access and sequencing of lemmas.

In Section 2, we addressed the issue of the representation of lexical and syntactic structure by examining the evidence from structural repetition priming studies. The data we (and many others) have reviewed provides evidence for the representation of abstract syntactic structures that is separate from both conceptual and lexical representations. These data speak against a radically incremental model of grammatical encoding driven purely by lexical syntax. Nevertheless, both conceptual representations (animacy, thematic roles) and lexical representations (verb subcategorisation information and biases) show independent effects on priming and can influence the generation of syntactic structure.

Regarding the effects of conceptual representation, it is clear that these representations must drive grammatical encoding processes, as the aim of grammatical encoding is to convey this information in language. However, current models of grammatical encoding make limited claims about the nature of conceptual representations involved. The production of grammatically acceptable sentences requires more information at the conceptual level than lexical concepts and their associated thematic roles (see Levelt, 1989). For example, the message should also encode information about the mood of the utterance to be produced in order to generate statements, questions or commands. Time, timing and place information should be represented for the appropriate grammatical encoding of tense, aspect and deixis. In addition, the grammatical encoder needs information about the utterance perspective, for example, the topic of the utterance, and what information is new or to be focused (essential in dialogue). Moreover, the nature of this information may differ based on language-specific grammatical requirements. Languages differ in what, and how, information must be encoded in order to produce a grammatical sentence (e.g., Slobin, 1982). For example, number in English is marked for singular and plural, whereas Arabic also marks the category dual. Such differences will have consequences not only for grammatical encoding processes cross-linguistically but also raise interesting questions about the nature of messages in bilinguals (and multilinguals) and their effect on first and second-language planning.

Current theories of grammatical encoding differ in how they model the links between conceptual representations and syntactic structure. As discussed in Section 3.1, the current evidence favours models that include direct links between conceptual and syntactic structures. However, more work is needed to build a detailed picture of this relationship. The lack of complexity at the message level is mirrored at the syntactic level in current theories. This is a result of the limited range and complexity of the sentence structures that have been tested. The vast majority of structural priming studies have focused on a few syntactic alternations in a relatively limited number of languages. This has, however, begun to change in recent years, with the advent of models incorporating sophisticated and detailed syntactic representations at both global and local levels of structure (e.g., Momma, 2021, 2022) based on studies testing encoding of more complex structures and syntactic dependencies. In addition, the clear requirement for comparative cross-linguistic data is driving the investigation of more numerous, and more diverse, languages (see Blasi et al., 2022, for a discussion).

The structural priming data in Section 2 also provide strong evidence for lexical contributions to syntactic structure generation. Some lexical effects can be short-lived (the lexical boost) compared to others (verb biases), and disagreement remains as to how best to model them. No current model can account for all aspects of the short-term and cumulative effects observed. Moreover, many models restrict lexical and structural interaction to verbs (Momma, 2021, 2022), despite evidence for the interactive effects with other lexical heads (e.g., nouns; Cleland & Pickering, 2003).

What is also clear from research in this field is that there is no steady state in terms of lexical and syntactic representations. An immense challenge for priming research is to link the effects of recent experience to learning effects more generally, both in terms of lifelong learning of a native language (e.g., Heyselaar, Wheeldon & Segaert, 2021) and the learning of second or third languages.

Lexical and syntactic contributions to the time-course of grammatical encoding were discussed in Section 3. Here the focus was on the degree to which lexical or syntactic representation drive the incremental planning of sentences. The evidence has obvious parallels with the structural priming results reviewed in Section 2. The role of syntactic structure in planning scope is evident in the data, once again arguing against Lexical Incrementality. Structural effects in planning have been shown for both local and distant (cross-clausal) syntactic dependencies. The data are thus more consistent with Hierarchical Incrementality involving the generation of abstract global syntactic structures prior to the sequential construction of local constituent phrases, although the precise coordination of these levels of planning remains to be determined.

The relationship between words and structure, in terms of processing scope, is also unclear. There is clearly an important role for verb retrieval in the generation of syntactic structure, albeit with limitations that are beginning to be clarified. The evidence also suggests that the scope of lexical retrieval is under the influence of, but is not fully determined by, syntactic structure. A complex range of interacting factors influence how many words we activate, retrieve and bind into a structure prior to speech onset. Some of these factors are non-linguistic, relating to cognitive load: the time-course of language production can be affected by processing demands within the grammatical encoding system but also by individual differences in working memory, attention and processing speed. It is also likely that different cognitive abilities have distinct effects for different components of the grammatical encoding process, and that these effects will also interact with different population characteristics such as language profiles (monolinguals and multilinguals) and age (younger and older adults).

Finally, the vast majority of experimental research on sentence production has (for very understandable reasons) elicited single sentences from speakers in non-interactive situations. However, the intention behind most of the language we produce is to convey information to others. The factors that have been shown to affect the time-course of grammatical encoding in monologue must also have consequences for dialogue. An important focus for future research is to determine how these consequences play out in interactive speaking situations, with all the additional linguistic complexity and cognitive demands that this entails.

References

Abdel-Rahman, R., & Melinger, A. (2009). Semantic context effects in language production: A swinging lexical network proposal and a review. *Language and Cognitive Processes, 24,* 713–34.

Allum, P. H., & Wheeldon, L. R. (2007). Planning scope in spoken sentence production: The role of grammatical units. *Journal of Experimental Psychology: Learning Memory and Cognition, 33,* 791–810.

Allum, P. H., & Wheeldon, L. R. (2009). Scope of lexical access in spoken sentence production: Implications for the conceptual-syntactic interface. *Journal of Experimental Psychology: Learning Memory and Cognition, 35,* 1240–55.

Balcetis, E. E., & Dale, R. (2005). An exploration of social modulation of syntactic priming. *Proceedings of the Annual Meeting of the Cognitive Science Society, 27*(27).

Barthel, M., & Sauppe, S. (2019). Speech planning at turn transitions in dialog is associated with increased processing load. *Cognitive Science, 43,* e12768.

Barthel, M., Sauppe, S., Levinson, S. C., & Meyer, A. S. (2016). The timing of utterance planning in task-oriented dialogue: Evidence from a novel list-completion paradigm. *Frontiers in Psychology, 7,* 1858.

Bernolet, S., Colleman, T., & Hartsuiker, R. J. (2014). The 'sense boost' to dative priming: Evidence for sense-specific verb-structure links. *Journal of Memory and Language, 76,* 113–26.

Bernolet, S., Collina, S., & Hartsuiker, R. J. (2016). The persistence of syntactic priming revisited. *Journal of Memory and Language, 91,* 99–116.

Bernolet, S., & Hartsuiker, R. J. (2010). Does verb bias modulate syntactic priming? *Cognition, 114,* 455–61.

Bernolet, S., Hartsuiker, R. J., & Pickering, M. J. (2007). Shared syntactic representations in bilinguals: Evidence for the role of word-order repetition. *Journal of Experimental Psychology: Learning, Memory, and Cognition, 33,* 931–49.

Bernolet, S., Hartsuiker, R. J., & Pickering, M. J. (2009). Persistence of emphasis in language production: A cross-linguistic approach. *Cognition, 112,* 300–17.

Bernolet, S., Hartsuiker, R. J., & Pickering, M. J. (2012). Effects of phonological feedback on the selection of syntax: Evidence from between-language syntactic priming. *Bilingualism: Language and Cognition, 15,* 503–16.

Bernolet, S., Hartsuiker, R. J., & Pickering, M. J. (2013). From language-specific to shared syntactic representations: The influence of second language proficiency on syntactic sharing in bilinguals. *Cognition, 127,* 287–306.

Blasi, D. E., Henrich, J., Adamou, E., Kemmerer, D., & Majid, A. (2022). Over-reliance on English hinders cognitive science. *Trends in Cognitive Sciences*, *26*(12), 1153–70.

Bock, J. K. (1982). Toward a cognitive psychology of syntax: Information processing contributions to sentence formulation. *Psychological Review*, *89*, 1–47.

Bock, J. K. (1986). Syntactic persistence in language production. *Cognitive Psychology*, *18*, 355–87.

Bock, J. K. (1987). Coordinating words and syntax in speech plans. In A. Ellis (Ed.), *Progress in the psychology of language*, Vol. 3 (pp. 337–90). London: Erlbaum.

Bock, K. (1989). Closed-class immanence in sentence production. *Cognition*, *31*, 163–86.

Bock, J. K., & Ferreira, V. S. (2014). Syntactically speaking. In M. Goldrick, V. S. Ferreira, & M. Miozzo (Eds.), *The Oxford handbook of language production* (pp. 21–46). Oxford: Oxford University Press.

Bock, K., & Cutting, J. C. (1992). Regulating mental energy: Performance units in language production. *Journal of Memory and Language*, *31*, 99–127.

Bock, K., Dell, G. S., Chang, F., & Onishi, K. H. (2007). Persistent structural priming from language comprehension to language production. *Cognition*, *104*, 437–58.

Bock, K., & Griffin, Z. M. (2000). The persistence of structural priming: Transient activation or implicit learning? *Journal of Experimental Psychology: General*, *129*, 177–92.

Bock, K., & Levelt, W. J. (1994). Language production: Grammatical encoding. In M. A. Gernsbacher (Ed.), *Handbook of psycholinguistics* (pp. 945–84). San Diego, CA: Academic Press.

Bock, K., & Loebell, H. (1990). Framing sentences. *Cognition*, *35*, 1–39.

Bock, K., Loebell, H., & Morey, R. (1992). From conceptual roles to structural relations: Bridging the syntactic cleft. *Psychological Review*, *99*, 150–71.

Branigan, H. (2007). Syntactic priming. *Language and Linguistics Compass*, *1*, 1–16.

Branigan, H. P., & Pickering, M. J. (2017). An experimental approach to linguistic representation. *Behavioral and Brain Sciences*, *40*, 1–73.

Branigan, H. P., Pickering, M. J., & Cleland, A. A. (2000). Syntactic co-ordination in dialogue. *Cognition*, *75*, B13–B25.

Branigan, H. P., Pickering, M. J., McLean, J. F., & Cleland, A. A. (2007). Syntactic alignment and participant role in dialogue. *Cognition*, *104*, 163–97.

Branigan, H. P., Pickering, M. J., McLean, J. F., & Stewart, A. J. (2006). The role of local and global syntactic structure in language production: Evidence from syntactic priming. *Language and Cognitive Processes*, *21*, 974–1010.

Branigan, H. P., Pickering, M. J., Pearson, J., & McLean, J. F. (2010). Linguistic alignment between people and computers. *Journal of Pragmatics, 42*, 2355–68.

Branigan, H. P., Pickering, M. J., & Tanaka, M. (2008). Contributions of animacy to grammatical function assignment and word order during production. *Lingua, 118*, 172–89.

Brown, R., & McNeill, D. (1966). The 'tip of the tongue' phenomenon. *Journal of Verbal Learning and Verbal Behavior, 5*(4), 325–37.

Brown-Schmidt, S., & Konopka, A. E. (2008). Little houses and casas pequeñas: Message formulation and syntactic form in unscripted speech with speakers of English and Spanish. *Cognition, 109*, 274–80.

Bunger, A., Papafragou, A., & Trueswell, J. C. (2013). Event structure influences language production: Evidence from structural priming in motion event description. *Journal of Memory and Language, 69*, 299–323.

Bürki, A., Elbuy, S., Madec, S., & Vasishth, S. (2020). What did we learn from forty years of research on semantic interference? A Bayesian meta-analysis. *Journal of Memory and Language, 114*, 104125.

Butterworth, B. (1980). Evidence from pauses in speech. In B. Butterworth (Ed.), *Language production: Vol. 1. Speech and talk* (pp. 155–76). London: Academic Press.

Cai, Z. G., Pickering, M. J., & Branigan, H. P. (2012). Mapping concepts to syntax: Evidence from structural priming in Mandarin Chinese. *Journal of Memory and Language, 66*, 833–49.

Caramazza, A., & Miozzo, M. (1997). The relation between syntactic and phonological knowledge in lexical access: Evidence from the tip-of-the-tongue phenomenon. *Cognition, 64*, 309–43.

Carminati, M. N., van Gompel, R. P., & Wakeford, L. J. (2019). An investigation into the lexical boost with nonhead nouns. *Journal of Memory and Language, 108*, 104031.

Chang, F. (2002). Symbolically speaking: A connectionist model of sentence production. *Cognitive Science, 26*, 609–51.

Chang, F., Bock, K., & Goldberg, A. E. (2003). Can thematic roles leave traces of their places? *Cognition, 90*, 29–49.

Chang, F., Dell, G. S., & Bock, K. J. (2006). Becoming syntactic. *Psychological Review, 113*, 234–72.

Chang, F., Janciauskas, M., & Fitz, H. (2012). Language adaptation and learning: Getting explicit about implicit learning. *Language and Linguistics Compass, 6*, 259–78.

Chomsky, N. (1965). *Aspects of the theory of syntax*. Cambridge, MA: MIT Press.

Christiansen, M. H., & Chater, N. (2016). The now-or-never bottleneck: A fundamental constraint on language. *Behavioral and Brain Sciences*, *39*, e62.

Christensen, P., Fusaroli, R., & Tylén, K. (2016). Environmental constraints shaping constituent order in emerging communication systems: Structural iconicity, interactive alignment and conventionalization. *Cognition*, *146*, 67–80.

Christianson, K., & Ferreira, F. (2005). Conceptual accessibility and sentence production in a free word order language (Odawa). *Cognition*, *98*, 105–35.

Clark, H. H., & Wilkes-Gibbs, D. (1986). Referring as a collaborative process. *Cognition*, *22*, 1–39.

Cleland, A. A., & Pickering, M. J. (2003). The use of lexical and syntactic information in language production: Evidence from the priming of noun-phrase structure. *Journal of Memory and Language*, *49*, 214–30.

Cleland, A. A., & Pickering, M. J. (2006). Do writing and speaking employ the same syntactic representations? *Journal of Memory and Language*, *54*, 185–98. http://dx.doi.org/10.1016/j.jml.2005.10.003.

Corps, R. E., Knudsen, B., & Meyer, A. S. (2022). Overrated gaps: Inter-speaker gaps provide limited information about the timing of turns in conversation. *Cognition*, *223*, 105037.

Coyle, J. M., & Kaschak, M. P. (2008). Patterns of experience with verbs affect long-term cumulative structural priming. *Psychonomic Bulletin & Review*, *15*, 967–70.

Cycowicz, Y. M., Friedman, D., Rothstein, M., Snodgrass, J.G. (1997) Picture naming by young children: norms for name agreement, familiarity, and visual complexity. *Journal of Experimental Child Psychology, 65* (2), 171–237.

Dell, G. S. (1986). A spreading-activation theory in sentence production. *Psychological Review*, *93*, 283–321.

Dell, G. S., & Chang, F. (2014). The P-chain: Relating sentence production and its disorders to comprehension and acquisition. *Philosophical Transactions of the Royal Society B: Biological Sciences*, *369*, 20120394.

Dell, G. S., & Jacobs, C. L. (2016). Successful speaking: Cognitive mechanisms of adaptation in language production. In G. Hickok and S. L. Small (Eds.), *Neurobiology of language* (pp. 209–19). San Diego, CA: Academic Press.

Dell, G. S., Nozari, N., & Oppenheim, G. M. (2014). Word production: Behavioral and computational considerations. In M. Goldrick, V. S. Ferreira, & M. Miozzo (Eds.), *The Oxford handbook of language production* (pp. 88–104). Oxford: Oxford University Press.

Dell, G. S., Oppenheim, G. M., & Kittredge, A. K. (2008). Saying the right word at the right time: Syntagmatic and paradigmatic interference in sentence production. *Language and Cognitive Processes*, *23*, 583–608.

Dell, G. S., Schwartz, M. F., Martin, N., Saffran, E. M., & Gagnon, D. A. (1997). Lexical access in aphasic and nonaphasic speakers. *Psychological Review*, *104*, 801–38.

Fairs, A., Bögels, S., & Meyer, A. S. (2018). Dual-tasking with simple linguistic tasks: Evidence for serial processing. *Acta Psychologica*, *191*, 131–48.

Fargier, R., & Laganaro, M. (2016). Neurophysiological modulations of non-verbal and verbal dual-tasks interference during word planning. *PLOS ONE*, *11*, e0168358.

Fehér, O., Wonnacott, E., & Smith, K. (2016). Structural priming in artificial languages and the regularisation of unpredictable variation. *Journal of Memory and Language*, *91*, 158–80.

Fellbaum, C. (2019). How flexible are idioms? A corpus-based study. *Linguistics*, *57*, 735–67.

Ferreira, F. (2000). Syntax in language production: An approach using tree-adjoining grammars. In L. Wheeldon (Ed.), *Aspects of language production* (pp. 291–330). San Diego, CA: Psychology Press.

Ferreira, F., & Swets, B. (2002). How incremental is language production? Evidence from the production of utterances requiring the computation of arithmetic sums. *Journal of Memory and Language*, *46*, 57–84.

Ferreira, V. S. (2003). The persistence of optional complementizer production: Why saying 'that' is not saying 'that' at all. *Journal of Memory and Language*, *48*, 379–98.

Ferreira, V. S., & Bock, K. (2006). The functions of structural priming. *Language and Cognitive Processes*, *21*, 1011–29.

Ferreira, V. S., Bock, K., Wilson, M. P., & Cohen, N. J. (2008). Memory for syntax despite amnesia. *Psychological Science*, *19*, 940–6.

Ferreira, V. S., Kleinman, D., Kraljic, T., & Siu, Y. (2012). Do priming effects in dialogue reflect partner-or task-based expectations? *Psychonomic Bulletin & Review*, *19*, 309–16.

Ferreira, V. S., Morgan, A., & Slevc, R. L. (2018). Grammatical encoding. In S.-A. Rueschemeyer & G. M. Gaskell (Eds.), *The Oxford handbook of psycholinguistics* (2nd ed., pp. 432–57). Oxford: Oxford University Press.

Ferreira, V. S., & Slevc, L. R. (2007). Grammatical encoding. In M. G. Gaskell (Ed.), *The Oxford handbook of psycholinguistics* (pp. 453–70). Oxford: Oxford University Press.

Fisher, C. (2002). The role of abstract syntactic knowledge in language acquisition: A reply to Tomasello (2000). *Cognition*, *82*, 259–78.

Fitz, H., & Chang, F. (2017). Meaningful questions: The acquisition of auxiliary inversion in a connectionist model of sentence production. *Cognition*, *166*, 225–50.

Fox Tree, J. E., & Meijer, P. J. A. (1999). Building syntactic structure in speaking. *Journal of Psycholinguistic Research, 28,* 71–92.

Frank, R. (2002). *Phrase structure composition and syntactic dependencies.* Cambridge, MA: MIT Press.

Fuchs, S., Petrone, C., Krivokapić, J., & Hoole, P. (2013). Acoustic and respiratory evidence for utterance planning in German. *Journal of Phonetics, 41,* 29–47.

Garrett, M. F. (1975). The analysis of sentence production. In *Psychology of learning and motivation: Advances in research and theory* (Vol. 9, Issue C, pp. 133–77). New York: Academic Press.

Garrett, M. F. (1980a). Levels of processing in sentence production. In B. Butterworth (Ed.), *Language production: Vol. 1. Speech and talk* (pp. 177–220). London: Academic Press.

Garrett, M. F. (1980b). The limits of accommodation: Arguments for independent processing levels in sentence production. In V. A. Fromkin (Ed.), *Errors in linguistic performance: Slips of the tongue, ear, pen and hand* (pp. 263–71). New York: Academic Press.

Gilbert, A. C., Cousineau-Perusse, M., & Titone, D. (2020). L2 exposure modulates the scope of planning during first and second language production. *Bilingualism: Language and Cognition, 23*(5), 1093–105.

Gleitman, L. R., January, D., Nappa, R., & Trueswell, J. C. (2007). On the give and take between event apprehension and utterance formulation. *Journal of Memory and Language, 57*(4), 544–69.

Goldman Eisler, F. (1968). *Psycholinguistics: Experiments in spontaneous speech.* New York: Academic Press.

Gollan, T. H., & Acenas, L. A. R. (2004). What is a TOT? Cognate and translation effects on tip-of-the-tongue states in Spanish-English and Tagalog-English bilinguals. *Journal of Experimental Psychology: Learning, Memory, and Cognition, 30,* 246–69.

Gries, S. T. (2005). Syntactic priming: A corpus-based approach. *Journal of Psycholinguistic Research, 34,* 365–99.

Griffin, Z. M. (2001). Gaze durations during speech reflect word selection and phonological encoding. *Cognition, 82,* 1–16.

Griffin, Z. M., & Bock, K. J. (2000). What the eyes say about speaking. *Psychological Science, 11,* 274–9.

Griffin, Z. M., & Davison, J. C. (2011). A technical introduction to using speakers' eye movements to study language. *The Mental Lexicon, 6,* 53–82.

Gruberg, N., Ostrand, R., Momma, S., & Ferreira, V. S. (2019). Syntactic entrainment: The repetition of syntactic structures in event descriptions. *Journal of Memory and Language, 107,* 216–32.

Hardy, S. M., Segaert, K., & Wheeldon, L. (2020). Healthy aging and sentence production: Disrupted lexical access in the context of intact syntactic planning. *Frontiers in Psychology, 11*, 257.

Hardy, S. M., Wheeldon, L., & Segaert, K. (2020). Structural priming is determined by global syntax rather than internal phrasal structure: Evidence from young and older adults. *Journal of Experimental Psychology: Learning, Memory, and Cognition, 46*, 720–40.

Hare, M. L., & Goldberg, A. E. (2000). Structural priming: purely syntactic? In M. Hahn & S. C. Stones (Eds.), *Proceedings of the twenty-first annual meeting of the Cognitive Science Society* (pp. 208–11), Mahwah, NJ: Lawrence Erlbaum Associates.

Hartsuiker, R. J., & Bernolet, S. (2017). The development of shared syntax in second language learning. *Bilingualism: Language and Cognition, 20*, 219–34.

Hartsuiker, R. J., Bernolet, S., Schoonbaert, S., Speybroeck, S., & Vanderelst, D. (2008). Syntactic priming persists while the lexical boost decays: Evidence from written and spoken dialogue. *Journal of Memory and Language, 58*, 214–38.

Hartsuiker, R. J., & Pickering, M. J. (2008). Language integration in bilingual sentence production. *Acta Psychologica, 128*, 479–89.

Hartsuiker, R. J., Pickering, M. J., & Veltkamp, E. (2004). Is syntax separate or shared between languages? Crosslinguistic syntactic priming in Spanish-English bilinguals. *Psychological Science, 15*, 409–14.

Heyselaar, E., Hagoort, P., & Segaert, K. (2017). In dialogue with an avatar, language behavior is identical to dialogue with a human partner. *Behavior Research Methods, 49*, 46–60.

Heyselaar, E., Segaert, K., Walvoort, S. J. W., Kessels, R. P. C., & Hagoort, P. (2017). The role of procedural memory in the skill for language: Evidence from syntactic priming inpatients with amnesia. *Neuropsychologia, 101*, 97–105.

Heyselaar, E., Wheeldon, L., & Segaert, K. (2021). Structural priming is supported by different components of nondeclarative memory: Evidence from priming across the lifespan. *Journal of Experimental Psychology: Learning, Memory, and Cognition*, 47, 820–37.

Huettig, F., Rommers, J., & Meyer, A. S. (2011). Using the visual world paradigm to study language processing: A review and critical evaluation. *Acta Psychologica, 137*, 151–71.

Hwang, H., & Chun, E. (2018). Influence of social perception and social monitoring on structural priming. *Cognitive Science, 42*, 303–13.

Hwang, H., & Kaiser, E. (2014a). Having a syntactic choice is not always better: The effects of syntactic flexibility on Korean production. *Language, Cognition and Neuroscience, 29*, 1115–31.

Hwang, H., & Kaiser, E. (2014b). The role of the verb in grammatical function assignment in English and Korean. *Journal of Experimental Psychology: Learning, Memory, and Cognition, 40,* 1363–73.

Hwang, H., & Kaiser, E. (2015). Accessibility effects on production vary cross-linguistically: Evidence from English and Korean. *Journal of Memory and Language, 84,* 190–204. https://doi.org/10.1016/j.jml.2015.06.004.

Hwang, H., & Shin, J. A. (2019). Cumulative effects of syntactic experience in a between- and a within-language context: Evidence for implicit learning. *Journal of Memory and Language, 109,* 104054.

Ivanova, I., Branigan, H. P., McLean, J. F., Costa, A., & Pickering, M. J. (2017) Do you what I say? People reconstruct the syntax of anomalous utterances. *Language, Cognition and Neuroscience 32,* 175–89.

Ivanova, I., Horton, W. S., Swets, B., Kleinman, D., & Ferreira, V. S. (2020). Structural alignment in dialogue and monologue (and what attention may have to do with it). *Journal of Memory and Language, 110,* 104052.

Ivanova, I., Pickering, M. J., Branigan, H. P., McLean, J. F., & Costa, A. (2012). The comprehension of anomalous sentences: Evidence from structural priming. *Cognition, 122,* 193–209.

Jackson, C. N. (2018). Second language structural priming: A critical review and directions for future research. *Second Language Research, 34,* 539–52.

Jackson, C. N., & Ruf, H. T. (2017). The priming of word order in second language German. *Applied Psycholinguistics, 38,* 315–45.

Jackson, C. N., & Ruf, H. T. (2018). The importance of prime repetition among intermediate-level second language learners. *Studies in Second Language Acquisition, 40,* 677–92.

Jaeger, T. F., & Snider, N. E. (2013). Alignment as a consequence of expectation adaptation: Syntactic priming is affected by the prime's prediction error given both prior and recent experience. *Cognition, 127,* 57–83.

Jongman, S. R., Meyer, A. S., & Roelofs, A. (2015). The role of sustained attention in the production of conjoined noun phrases: An individual differences study. *PLOS ONE, 10,* e0137557.

Jongman, S. R., Roelofs, A., & Meyer, A. S. (2015). Sustained attention in language production: An individual differences investigation. *Quarterly Journal of Experimental Psychology, 68,* 710–30.

Kaan, E., & Chun, E. (2018). Priming and adaptation in native speakers and second-language learners. *Bilingualism: Language and Cognition, 21,* 228–42.

Karimi, H., & Ferreira, F. (2016). Good-enough linguistic representations and online cognitive equilibrium in language processing. *Quarterly Journal of Experimental Psychology, 69,* 1013–40.

Kaschak, M. P. (2007). Long-term structural priming affects subsequent patterns of language production. *Memory & Cognition, 35*, 925–37.

Kaschak, M. P., & Borreggine, K. L. (2008). Is long-term structural priming affected by patterns of experience with individual verbs? *Journal of Memory and Language, 58*, 862–78.

Kaschak, M. P., Kutta, T. J., & Schatschneider, C. (2011). Long-term cumulative structural priming persists for (at least) one week. *Memory & Cognition, 39*, 381–8.

Kaschak, M. P., Loney, R. A., & Borreggine, K. L. (2006). Recent experience affects the strength of structural priming. *Cognition, 99*, B73–B82.

Kempen, G., & Hoenkamp, E. (1987). An incremental procedural grammar for sentence formulation. *Cognitive Science, 11*, 201–58.

Kempen, G., & Huijbers, P. (1983). The lexicalization process in sentence production and naming: Indirect election of words. *Cognition, 14*, 185–209.

Khoe, Y. H., Tsoukala, C., Kootstra, G. J., & Frank, S. L. (2021). Is structural priming between different languages a learning effect? Modelling priming as error-driven implicit learning. *Language, Cognition and Neuroscience*, 1–21.

Konopka, A. E. (2012). Planning ahead: How recent experience with structures and words changes the scope of linguistic planning. *Journal of Memory and Language, 66*, 143–62.

Konopka, A. E. (2019). Encoding actions and verbs: Tracking the time-course of relational encoding during message and sentence formulation. *Journal of Experimental Psychology: Learning, Memory, and Cognition, 45*, 1486–510.

Konopka, A. E., & Bock, J. K. (2005). Helping syntax out: How much do words do? Paper presented at the 18th CUNY Human Sentence Processing Conference (CUNY 2005), Arizona, United States.

Konopka, A. E., & Bock, K. (2009). Lexical or syntactic control of sentence formulation? Structural generalizations from idiom production. *Cognitive Psychology, 58*, 68–101.

Konopka, A. E., & Brown-Schmidt, S. (2014). Message encoding. In M. Goldrick, V. S. Ferreira, & M. Miozzo (Eds.), *The Oxford handbook of language production* (pp. 3–20). Oxford: Oxford University Press.

Konopka, A. E., & Kuchinsky, S. E. (2015). How message similarity shapes the timecourse of sentence formulation. *Journal of Memory and Language, 84*, 1–23.

Konopka, A. E., & Meyer, A. S. (2014). Priming sentence planning. *Cognitive Psychology, 73*, 1–40.

Konopka, A. E., Meyer, A. S., & Forest, T. A. (2018). Planning to speak in L1 and L2. *Cognitive Psychology, 102,* 72–104.

Kootstra, G. J., & Doedens, W. J. (2016). How multiple sources of experience influence bilingual syntactic choice: Immediate and cumulative cross-language effects of structural priming, verb bias, and language dominance. *Bilingualism: Language and Cognition, 19,* 710–32.

Kuchinsky, S. E., & Bock, K. (2010). *From seeing to saying: Perceiving, planning, producing.* Paper presented at the 23rd meeting of the CUNY Human Sentence Processing Conference, New York, NY.

Lee, E. K., Brown-Schmidt, S., & Watson, D. G. (2013). Ways of looking ahead: Hierarchical planning in language production. *Cognition, 129,* 544–62.

Levelt, W. J. M. (1989). *Speaking: From intention to articulation.* Cambridge, MA: MIT Press.

Levelt, W. J. M. (1992). Accessing words in speech production: Stages, processes and representations. *Cognition, 42,* 1–22.

Levelt, W. J., & Kelter, S. (1982). Surface form and memory in question answering. *Cognitive Psychology, 14,* 78–106.

Levelt, W. J. M., & Maassen, B. (1981). Lexical search and order of mention in sentence production. In W. Klein & W. J. M. Levelt (Eds.), *Crossing the boundaries in linguistics* (pp. 221–52). Dortrecht: Reidel.

Levelt, W. J. M., & Meyer, A. S. (2000). Word for word: Multiple lexical access in speech production. *The European Journal of Cognitive Psychology, 12,* 433–52.

Levelt, W. J., Roelofs, A., & Meyer, A. S. (1999). A theory of lexical access in speech production. *Behavioral and Brain Sciences, 22,* 1–38.

Levinson, S. C., & Torreira, F. (2015). Timing in turn-taking and its implications for processing models of language. *Frontiers in Psychology, 6,* 731.

Li, C., Ferreira, V. S., & Gollan, T. H. (2022). Language control after phrasal planning: Playing whack-a-mole with language switch costs. *Journal of Memory and Language, 126,* 104338.

Lindsay, L., Gambi, C., & Rabagliati, H. (2019). Preschoolers optimize the timing of their conversational turns through flexible coordination of language comprehension and production. *Psychological Science, 30,* 504–15.

Loebell, H., & Bock, K. (2003). Structural priming across languages. *Linguistics, 41,* 791–824.

Mahon, B. Z., Costa, A., Peterson, R., Vargas, K. A., & Caramazza, A. (2007). Lexical selection is not by competition: A reinterpretation of semantic interference and facilitation effects in the picture-word interference paradigm. *Journal of Experimental Psychology: Learning, Memory, and Cognition, 33*(3), 503–35.

Mahowald, K., James, A., Futrell, R., & Gibson, E. (2016). A meta-analysis of syntactic priming in language production. *Journal of Memory and Language*, *91*, 5–27.

Malpass, D., & Meyer, A. S. (2010). The time course of name retrieval during multiple-object naming: Evidence from extrafoveal-on-foveal effects. *Journal of Experimental Psychology: Learning, Memory, and Cognition*, *36*(2), 523–37.

Martin, R. C. (2021). The critical role of semantic working memory in language processing. *Current Directions in Psychological Science*, *30*, 283–91.

Martin, R. C., Crowther, J. E., Knight, M., Tamborello, F. P., & Yang, C. L. (2010). Planning in sentence production: Evidence for the phrase as a default planning scope. *Cognition*, *116*, 177–92.

Martin, R. C., & Freedman, M. L. (2001). Short-term retention of lexical-semantic representations: Implications for speech production. *Memory*, *9*(4–6), 261–80.

Martin, R. C., Miller, M., & Vu, H. (2004). Lexical-semantic retention and speech production: Further evidence from normal and brain-damaged participants for a phrasal scope of planning. level. *Cognitive Neuropsychology*, *21*, 625–44.

Martin, R. C., & Schnur, T. T. (2019). Independent contributions of semantic and phonological working memory to spontaneous speech in acute stroke. *Cortex*, *112*, 58–68.

Martin, R. C., & Slevc, L. R. (2014). Language production and working memory. In M. Goldrick, V. S. Ferreria, & M. Miozzo (Eds.), *The Oxford handbook of language production* (pp. 120–31). Oxford: Oxford University Press.

Martin, R. C., Yan, H., & Schnur, T. T. (2014). Working memory and planning during sentence production. *Acta Psychologica*, *152*, 120–32.

Melinger, A., & Dobel, C. (2005). Lexically-driven syntactic priming. *Cognition*, *98*, B11–B20.

Messenger, K., Branigan, H. P., & McLean, J. F. (2011). Evidence for (shared) abstract structure underlying children's short and full passives. *Cognition*, *121*, 268–74.

Messenger, K., Branigan, H. P., McLean, J. F., & Sorace, A. (2012). Is young children's passive syntax semantically constrained? Evidence from syntactic priming. *Journal of Memory and Language*, *66*, 568–87.

Meyer, A. S. (1996). Lexical access in phrase and sentence production: Results from picture-word interference experiments. *Journal of Memory and Language*, *35*, 477–96.

Meyer, A. S., & Bock, K. (1992). The tip-of-the-tongue phenomenon: Blocking or partial activation? *Memory & Cognition*, *20*(6), 715–26.

Meyer, A. S., Sleiderink, A. M., & Levelt, W. J. M. (1998). Viewing and naming objects: Eye movements during noun phrase production. *Cognition*, *66*, B25–B33.

Meyer, A. S., Wheeldon, L., Van der Meulen, F., & Konopka, A. (2012). Effects of speech rate and practice on the allocation of visual attention in multiple object naming. *Frontiers in Psychology*, *3*, 39.

Miyake, A., Friedman, N. P., Emerson, M. J. et al. (2000). The unity and diversity of executive functions and their contributions to complex 'frontal lobe' tasks: A latent variable analysis. *Cognitive Psychology*, *41*, 49–100.

Momma, S. (2021). Filling the gap in gap-filling: Long-distance dependency formation in sentence production. *Cognitive Psychology*, *129*, 101411.

Momma, S. (2022). Producing filler-gap dependencies: Structural priming evidence for two distinct combinatorial processes in production. *Journal of Memory and Language*, *126*, 104349.

Momma, S., Buffinton, J., Slevc, L. R., & Phillips, C. (2020). Syntactic category constrains lexical competition in speaking. *Cognition*, *197*, 104183.

Momma, S., & Ferreira., V. (2021). Beyond linear order: The role of argument structure in speaking. *Cognitive Psychology*, *128*, 101397.

Momma, S., & Phillips, C. (2018). The relationship between parsing and generation. *Annual Review of Linguistics*, *4*, 233–54.

Momma, S., Slevc, L., & Phillips, C. (2015). The timing of verb planning in active and passive sentence production. Poster presented at the 28th annual CUNY conference on Human Sentence Processing.

Momma, S., Slevc, L. R., & Phillips, C. (2016). The timing of verb selection in Japanese sentence production. *Journal of Experimental Psychology: Learning, Memory, and Cognition*, *42*, 813–24.

Momma, S., Slevc, L. R., & Phillips, C. (2018). Unaccusativity in sentence production. *Linguistic Inquiry*, *49*, 181–94.

Morgan, J. L., & Meyer, A. S. (2005). Processing of extrafoveal objects during multiple object naming. *Journal of Experimental Psychology: Learning, Memory, and Cognition*, 31, 428–42.

Myachykov, A., Garrod, S., & Scheepers, C. (2010). Perceptual priming of structural choice during English and Finnish sentence production. In R. K. Mishra and N. Srinivasan (Eds.), *Language & cognition: State of the art* (pp. 54–72). Munich: Lincom Europa.

Myachykov, A., Garrod, S., & Scheepers, C. (2018). Attention and memory play different roles in syntactic choice during sentence production. *Discourse Processes*, *55*, 218–29.

Myachykov, A., Scheepers, C., Garrod, S., Thompson, D., & Fedorova, O. (2013). Syntactic flexibility and competition in sentence production: The case of English and Russian. *Quarterly Journal of Experimental Psychology*, *66*, 1601–19.

Myachykov, A., Thompson, D., Scheepers, C., & Garrod, S. (2011). Visual attention and structural choice in sentence production across languages. *Language and Linguistics Compass*, *5*, 95–107.

Myachykov, A., & Tomlin, R. S. (2008). Perceptual priming and structural choice in Russian sentence production. *Journal of Cognitive Science*, *6*, 31–48.

Norcliffe, E., & Konopka, A. E. (2015). Vision and language in cross-linguistic research on sentence production. In R. K. Mishra, N. Srinivasan, & F. Huettig (Eds.), *Attention and vision in language processing* (pp. 77–96). New York: Springer.

Norcliffe, E., Konopka, A. E., Brown, P., & Levinson, S. C. (2015). Word order affects the time course of sentence formulation in Tzeltal. *Language, Cognition and Neuroscience*, *30*, 1187–208.

Oppenheim, G. M., Dell, G. S., & Schwartz, M. F. (2010). The dark side of incremental learning: A model of cumulative semantic interference during lexical access in speech production. *Cognition*, *114*, 227–52.

Oppenheim, G. M., & Nozari, N. (2021). Behavioral interference or facilitation does not distinguish between competitive and noncompetitive accounts of lexical selection in word production. *Proceedings of the Annual Meeting of the Cognitive Science Society*, *43*, 625–31.

Peter, M., Chang, F., Pine, J. M., Blything, R., & Rowland, C. F. (2015). When and how do children develop knowledge of verb argument structure? Evidence from verb bias effects in a structural priming task. *Journal of Memory and Language*, *81*, 1–15.

Petrone, C., Fuchs, S., & Krivovokapić, J. (2011). Consequences of working memory differences and phrasal length on pause duration and fundamental frequency. In *Proceedings of the 9th International Seminar on Speech Production (Montréal, QC)* (pp. 393–400).

Piai, V., & Roelofs, A. (2013). Working memory capacity and dual-task interference in picture naming. *Acta Psychologica*, *142*, 332–42.

Pickering, M. J., & Branigan, H. P. (1998). The representation of verbs: Evidence from syntactic priming in language production. *Journal of Memory and Language*, *39*, 633–51.

Pickering, M. J., & Ferreira, V. S. (2008). Structural priming: A critical review. *Psychological Bulletin*, *134*, 427–59.

Pickering, M. J., & Garrod, S. (2004). Toward a mechanistic psychology of dialogue. *Behavioral and Brain Sciences*, *27*, 169–90.

Prat-Sala, M., & Branigan, H. P. (2000). Discourse constraints on syntactic processing in language production: A cross-linguistic study in English and Spanish. *Journal of Memory and Language*, *42*, 168–82.

Reitter, D., Keller, F., & Moore, J. D. (2011). A computational cognitive model of syntactic priming. *Cognitive Science, 35,* 587–637.

Reitter, D., & Moore, J. D. (2014). Alignment and task success in spoken dialogue. *Journal of Memory and Language, 76,* 29–46.

Roberts, S. G., Torreira, F., & Levinson, S. C. (2015). The effects of processing and sequence organization on the timing of turn taking: A corpus study. *Frontiers in Psychology, 6,* 509.

Roelofs, A. (1992). A spreading-activation theory of lemma retrieval in speaking. *Cognition, 42*(1–3), 107–42. https://doi.org/10.1016/0010-0277(92)90041-F.

Roelofs, A., & Ferreira, V. S. (2019). The architecture of speaking. In P. Hagoort (Ed.), *Human language: From genes and brains to behavior* (pp. 35–50). Cambridge, MA: MIT Press.

Roelofs, A., Meyer, A. S., & Levelt, W. J. M. (1998). A case for the lemma/lexeme distinction in models of speaking: Comment on Caramazza and Miozzo (1997). *Cognition, 69,* 219–30.

Roelofs, A., & Piai, V. (2011). Attention demands of spoken word planning: A review. *Frontiers in Psychology, 2,* 307.

Roeser, J., Torrance, M. C., & Baguley, T. S. (2019). Advance planning in written and spoken sentence production. *Journal of Experimental Psychology: Learning, Memory, and Cognition, 11,* 1993–2009.

Rowland, C. F., Chang, F., Ambridge, B., Pine, J. M., & Lieven, E. V. (2012). The development of abstract syntax: Evidence from structural priming and the lexical boost. *Cognition, 125,* 49–63.

Salamoura, A., & Williams, J. N. (2006). Lexical activation of cross-language syntactic priming. *Bilingualism: Language and Cognition, 9,* 299–307.

Santesteban, M., Pickering, M. J., & McLean, J. F. (2010). Lexical and phonological effects on syntactic processing: Evidence from syntactic priming. *Journal of Memory and Language, 63,* 347–66.

Sarvasy, H. S., Morgan, A. M., Yu, J., Ferreira, V., & Momma, S. (2022). Cross-clause planning in Nungon (Papua New Guinea): Eye-tracking evidence. *Memory & Cognition, 1,* 1–15.

Sauppe, S., Norcliffe, E., Konopka, A. E., Van Valin, R. D., & Levinson, S. C. (2013). Dependencies first: Eye tracking evidence from sentence production in Tagalog. In *Proceedings of the Annual Meeting of the Cognitive Science Society, 35*(35), 1265–70.

Scheepers, C., Raffray, C. N., & Myachykov, A. (2017). The lexical boost effect is not diagnostic of lexically-specific syntactic representations. *Journal of Memory and Language, 95,* 102–15.

Scheepers, C., & Sturt, P. (2014). Bidirectional syntactic priming across cognitive domains: From arithmetic to language and back. *Quarterly Journal of Experimental Psychology, 67,* 1643–54.

Scheepers, C., Sturt, P., Martin, C. J. et al. (2011). Structural priming across cognitive domains: From simple arithmetic to relative-clause attachment. *Psychological Science, 22,* 1319–26.

Schoonbaert, S., Hartsuiker, R. J., & Pickering, M. J. (2007). The representation of lexical and syntactic information in bilinguals: Evidence from syntactic priming. *Journal of Memory and Language, 56,* 153–71.

Schoot, L., Hagoort, P., & Segaert, K. (2019). Stronger syntactic alignment in the presence of an interlocutor. *Frontiers in Psychology, 10,* 685.

Schlenter, J., Esaulova, Y., Dolscheid, S., & Penke, M. (2022). Ambiguity in case marking does not affect the description of transitive events in German: Evidence from sentence production and eye-tracking. *Language, Cognition and Neuroscience, 37,* 844–65.

Schotter, E. R., Ferreira, V. S., & Rayner, K. (2013). Parallel object activation and attentional gating of information: Evidence from eye movements in the multiple object naming paradigm. *Journal of Experimental Psychology: Learning, Memory, and Cognition, 39,* 365–74.

Schriefers, H., Meyer, A. S., & Levelt, W. J. M. (1990). Exploring the time course of lexical access in language production: Picture-word interference studies. *Journal of Memory and Language, 29,* 86–102.

Schriefers, H., Teruel, E., and Meinshausen, R. M. (1998). Producing simple sentences: Results from picture-word interference experiments. *Journal of Memory and Language, 39,* 609–32.

Segaert, K., Lucas, S. J. E., Burley, C. V. et al. (2018). Higher physical fitness levels are associated with less language decline in healthy ageing. *Scientific Reports, 8,* 6715.

Segaert, K., Weber, K., Cladder-Micus, M., & Hagoort, P. (2014). The influence of verb-bound syntactic preferences on the processing of syntactic structures. *Journal of Experimental Psychology: Learning, Memory, and Cognition, 40,* 1448–60.

Segaert, K., Wheeldon, L., & Hagoort, P. (2016). Unifying structural priming effects on syntactic choices and timing of sentence generation. *Journal of Memory and Language, 91,* 59–80.

Shao, Z., Roelofs, A., & Meyer, A. S. (2012). Sources of individual differences in the speed of naming objects and actions: The contribution of executive control. *Quarterly Journal of Experimental Psychology, 65,* 1927–44.

Sjerps, M. J., & Meyer, A. S. (2015). Variation in dual-task performance reveals late initiation of speech planning in turn-taking. *Cognition, 136,* 304–24.

Slobin, D. (1982). Universal and particular in the acquisition of language. In E. Wanner & L. Gleitman (Eds.), *Language acquisition: The state of the art* (pp. 128–72). New York: Cambridge University Press.

Smith, M. C. (2000). Conceptual structures in language production. In L. Wheeldon (Ed.), *Aspects of language production* (pp. 331–74). Hove: Psychology Press.

Smith, M., & Wheeldon, L. R. (1999). High level processing scope in spoken sentence production. *Cognition, 73*, 205–46.

Smith, M., & Wheeldon, L. (2001). Syntactic priming in spoken sentence production: An online study. *Cognition, 78*(2), 123–64.

Smith, M., & Wheeldon, L. R. (2004). Horizontal information flow in spoken sentence production. *Journal of Experimental Psychology: Learning, Memory and Cognition, 30*, 675–86.

Steedman, M. (2000). *The syntactic process.* Cambridge, MA: MIT Press.

Suffill, E., Kutasi, T., Pickering, M. J., & Branigan, H. P. (2021). Lexical alignment is affected by addressee but not speaker nativeness. *Bilingualism: Language and Cognition, 24*, 746–57.

Swets, B., Desmet, T., Hambrick, D. Z., & Ferreira, F. (2007). The role of working memory in syntactic ambiguity resolution: A psychometric approach. *Journal of Experimental Psychology: General, 136*(1), 64–81.

Swets, B., Fuchs, S., Krivokapić, J., & Petrone, C. (2021). A cross-linguistic study of individual differences in speech planning. *Frontiers in Psychology, 12*, 655516.

Swets, B., Jacovina, M. E., & Gerrig, R. J. (2014). Individual differences in the scope of speech planning: Evidence from eye-movements. *Language and Cognition, 6*, 12–44.

Tanaka, M. N., Branigan, H. P., McLean, J. F., & Pickering, M. J. (2011). Conceptual influences on word order and voice in sentence production: Evidence from Japanese. *Journal of Memory and Language, 65*, 318–30.

Tomasello, M. (2000). The item-based nature of children's early syntactic development. *Trends in Cognitive Sciences, 4*, 156–63.

Tooley, K. M., & Bock, K. (2014). On the parity of structural persistence in language production and comprehension. *Cognition, 132*, 101–36.

Torreira, F., Bögels, S., & Levinson, S. C. (2015). Breathing for answering: The time course of response planning in conversation. *Frontiers in Psychology, 6*, 284.

van Gompel, R. P., & Arai, M. (2018). Structural priming in bilinguals. *Bilingualism: Language and Cognition, 21*, 448–55.

van Gompel, R. P., Wakeford, L. J., & Kantola, L. (2022). No looking back: The effects of visual cues on the lexical boost in structural priming. *Language, Cognition and Neuroscience*, *38*, 1–10.

van de Cavey, J., & Hartsuiker, R. J. (2016). Is there a domain-general cognitive structuring system? Evidence from structural priming across music, math, action descriptions, and language. *Cognition*, *146*, 172–84.

van de Velde, M., Meyer, A. S., & Konopka, A. E. (2014). Message formulation and structural assembly: Describing 'easy' and 'hard' events with preferred and dispreferred syntactic structures. *Journal of Memory and Language*, *71*, 124–44.

Wagner, V., Jescheniak, J. D., & Schriefers, H. (2010). On the flexibility of grammatical advance planning during sentence production: Effects of cognitive load on multiple lexical access. *Journal of Experimental Psychology: Learning, Memory, and Cognition*, *36*, 423–40.

Weatherholtz, K., Campbell-Kibler, K., & Jaeger, T. F. (2014). Socially-mediated syntactic alignment. *Language Variation and Change*, *26*, 387–420.

Wheeldon, L. (2011). Generating spoken sentences: The relationship between words and syntax. *Language and Linguistic Compass*, *5*, 310–21.

Wheeldon, L. R. (2013). Producing spoken sentences: The scope of incremental planning. In S. Fuchs, M. Weirich, D. Pape, & P. Perrier (Eds.), *Speech production and perception: Vol. 1. Speech planning and dynamics* (pp. 97–118). Frankfurt: Peter Lang.

Wheeldon, L. R., & Konopka, A. (2018). Spoken word production: Representation, retrieval, and integration. In S-A. Rueschemeyer & M. G. Gaskell (Eds.), *The Oxford handbook of psycholinguistics* (pp. 335–71). Oxford: Oxford University Press.

Wheeldon, L., & Lahiri, A. (1997). Prosodic units in speech production. *Journal of Memory and Language*, *37*, 356–81.

Wheeldon, L. R., & Lahiri, A. (2002). The minimal unit of phonological encoding: Prosodic or lexical word. *Cognition*, *85*, B31–B41.

Wheeldon, L. R., & Meyer, A. (2005). Planning sentence structure: Speech latency and gaze patterns during the production of word lists and sentence. Paper presented at the 4th Workshop on Language Production, Maastricht.

Wheeldon, L. R., Ohlson, N., Ashby, A., & Gator, S. (2013). Lexical availability and grammatical encoding scope during spoken sentence production. *Quarterly Journal of Experimental Psychology*, *66*, 1653–73.

Wheeldon, L. R., & Smith, M. C. (2003). Phrase structure priming: A short-lived effect. *Language and Cognitive Processes*, *18*, 431–42.

Wheeldon, L. R., Smith, M. C., & Apperly, I. (2011). Repeating words in sentences: Effects of sentence structure. *Journal of Experimental Psychology: Learning, Memory, and Cognition, 37,* 1051–64.

Whittlesea, B. W., & Wright, R. L. (1997). Implicit (and explicit) learning: Acting adaptively without knowing the consequences. *Journal of Experimental Psychology: Learning, Memory, and Cognition, 23,* 181–200.

Wilson, V. A., Zuberbühler, K., & Bickel, B. (2022). The evolutionary origins of syntax: Event cognition in nonhuman primates. *Science Advances, 8*(25), eabn8464.

Wynne, H. S., Wheeldon, L., & Lahiri, A. (2018). Compounds, phrases and clitics in connected speech. *Journal of Memory and Language, 98,* 45–58.

Yan, H., Martin, R. C., & Slevc, L. R. (2018). Lexical overlap increases syntactic priming in aphasia independently of short-term memory abilities: Evidence against the explicit memory account of the lexical boost. *Journal of Neurolinguistics, 48,* 76–89.

Zhang, C., Bernolet, S., & Hartsuiker, R. J. (2020). The role of explicit memory in syntactic persistence: Effects of lexical cueing and load on sentence memory and sentence production. *PLOS ONE, 15,* e0240909.

Zhao, L. M., Alario, F. X., & Yang, Y. F. (2014). Grammatical planning scope in sentence production: Further evidence for the functional phrase hypothesis. *Applied Psycholinguistics, 36,* 1059–75.

Ziegler, J., Bencini, G., Goldberg, A., & Snedeker, J. (2019). How abstract is syntax? Evidence from structural priming. *Cognition, 193,* 104045.

Ziegler, J., & Snedeker, J. (2018). How broad are thematic roles? Evidence from structural priming. *Cognition, 179,* 221–40.

Ziegler, J., Snedeker, J., & Wittenberg, E. (2017). Event structures drive semantic structural priming, not thematic roles: Evidence from idioms and light verbs. *Cognitive Science, 42,* 2918–49.

Cambridge Elements ⹄

Psycholinguistics

Paul Warren
Victoria University of Wellington

Paul Warren is Professor of Linguistics at Victoria University of Wellington, where his teaching and research is in psycholinguistics, phonetics, and laboratory phonology. His publications include *Introducing Psycholinguistics* (2012) and *Uptalk* (2016), both published by CUP. He is a founding member of the Association for Laboratory Phonology, and a member of the Australasian Speech Science Technology Association and the International Phonetic Association. Paul is a member of the editorial boards for *Laboratory Phonology* and the *Journal of the International Phonetic Association*, and for twenty years (2000–2019) served on the editorial board of *Language and Speech*.

About the Series

This Elements series presents theoretical and empirical studies in the interdisciplinary field of psycholinguistics. Topics include issues in the mental representation and processing of language in production and comprehension, and the relationship of psycholinguistics to other fields of research. Each Element is a high quality and up-to-date scholarly work in a compact, accessible format.

Cambridge Elements ☰

Psycholinguistics

Elements in the Series

Verbal Irony Processing
Stephen Skalicky

Grammatical Encoding for Speech Production
Linda Ruth Wheeldon and Agnieszka Konopka

A full series listing is available at: www.cambridge.org/EPSL

Printed in the United States
by Baker & Taylor Publisher Services